A Retrospect on
The Dust-Laden History

THE PAST AND PRESENT OF TEKONG ISLAND IN SINGAPORE

A Retrospect on
The Dust-Laden
History

THE PAST AND PRESENT OF
TEKONG ISLAND IN SINGAPORE

Chen Poh Seng

Graduate from Nanyang University, Singapore

Lee Leong Sze

National Kaohsiung Normal University, Taiwan

 **World Scientific**

W JERSEY • LONDON • SINGAPORE • BEIJING • SHANGHAI • HONG KONG • TAIPEI • CHENNAI

Published by

World Scientific Publishing Co. Pte. Ltd.

5 Toh Tuck Link, Singapore 596224

USA office: 27 Warren Street, Suite 401-402, Hackensack, NJ 07601

UK office: 57 Shelton Street, Covent Garden, London WC2H 9HE

British Library Cataloguing-in-Publication Data
A catalogue record for this book is available from the British Library.

ISBN-13 978-981-4365-96-3 (pbk)
ISBN-10 981-4365-96-3 (pbk)

In-house Editor: Ms. Dan Jun

Typeset by Stallion Press
Email: enquiries@stallionpress.com

Printed in Singapore.

Preface by Chen Poh Seng

...ated in the northeastern sea of Singapore, Tekong Island is the largest ...shore island of Singapore. Due to its position, Tekong Island was once ...mportant thoroughfare point when ferry boats and ships were important ...les of transportation. During its peak, there were up to 5000 residents ...Tekong Island. My parents made their living on the island. My great ...ndfather, Chen Bing Kui (陈炳奎), was one of the founders of the earliest ...rate organization on the island, Guangdong & Fujian Association (粤闽馆) ...my grandfather succeeded his father's will to be a leader of the Tekong ...nd residents. My family was also closely connected with Oi Wah School ...华学校) and Chung Kong School (中光学校). However, my father, Chen Sit ...ang (陈锡漳) and his brothers, including my uncle Chin Sit Har (陈锡霞), ...the island when they became adults and earned their living in Johore ...aru and Changi Village in Singapore.

My maternal grandfather, Li Yun Lin (李云林) made tofu next to the ...n-air cinema and sold it in the market. My eldest uncle, Le Sun Hua ...森华), was educated in China where he studied in junior high school; ...er he taught Chinese martial arts on the island. My second uncle, Li Shun ...a (李顺华), succeeded his father's business and ran the tofu store. My ...ond aunt, Li Yue Hua (李月华), moved to Kampong Sanyongkong Parit ...er marrying Zhang Fo Tong (张佛同). My aunt's husband was good at ...nstructing *Kelong*, and I often played around it when I was a child. I ...d about 50 cousins, and most of them were born and educated in Tekong ...and.

Changi point was the only way to take the ferry boat to Tekong Island. ...ery year, when it was the time to worship the ancestors on Tomb-Sweeping ...y, my uncle bring my cousins to our home and we together took the boat ...the Chinese Cemetery on Tekong Island. In the early times, we walked ...to the hill from Selabin and later we would take a private taxi and tour ...und the island. Once in a while my mother would take me and my sister ...ck to Tekong Island to visit relatives in lunar December, and we watched ...e opera held to offer thanks to God. My relatives sent their children who ...anned to study further in Singapore to stay in my home. My cousin, Wu ...eng Jiao (吴梦蛟), Wu Te Qing (吴特青), Dr Ng Yin Kwee (吴应贵), and ...y uncle Lai Nan Shan (赖南山) first came to my home.

After I enrolled in the Department of Geography of Nanyang Universi‍ I assisted professor Zhou Bao Jun (邹豹君) to undertake a survey on Teko‍ Island. Another professor Sha Xue Jun (沙学俊), asked his students to ma‍ a map-reading report based on the military map on Tekong Island, Sc‍ 1:25,000. This assignment again shortened the distance between Teko‍ Island. Unfortunately, I lost the report.

On lunar January 1 of every year, I would drive my parents to worsh‍ God in Tian Kong Buddhist Temple in Bedok North and, as a result, w‍ acquainted with the secretary of the temple, Ho Kim Fong (何金煌). I re‍ Ho's work *History of Pulau Tekong & Tian Kong Buddhist Temple* a‍ thus I came up with an idea to investigate and explore the history of Teko‍ Island, which I am familiar with but do not understand deeply, by conducti‍ academic research.

The theme of Singapore Society of Asian Studies in 2004 was "Fo‍ Culture & Chinese Society." I found that the papers concerned with t‍ dialects in Singapore lacked that of the Hakka group. I met a Hakk‍ descendent, Lee Leong Sze (利亮时) by introduction from the society President Lee Guan Kin. By cooperating with Lee, we completed t‍ paper *Relationship between Hakkas Community and Grand Uncle Belief – Example for Singapore and Malaysia Hakka Community*. Later, I mentione‍ to Lee that I planned to explore the history of Tekong Island, and we share‍ the same view on this research.

My appreciation goes to those who were helpful in the realization of th‍ research (more detail in the preface by Lee Leong Sze). The publication c‍ the English version was not my original intention; yet it was the result c‍ the endeavor of many people. Hereby I would like to dedicate this book t‍ all the residents of Tekong Island and their descendents.

Preface by Lee Leong Sze

...ally, the English version of *A Retrospect on the Dust-laden History: Past and Present of Tekong Island in Singapore* is being published. In ...gust 2005, Chen Poh Seng (陈波生), who is also a member of the Society ...Asian Studies, approached me and mentioned his interest in studying ...ong Island. Soon we shared the same views on conducting this research ...prepared the proposal and were looking for sponsors. With Mr. Chen's ...eavor, we were lucky that Mr. Ho Kiau Seng (何侨生), Mr. Chen Ting (陈廷雷) and Mr. Lu He Nan (吕河南) promised to sponsor our research ...he project was started in the beginning of 2007.

Before conducting this study, I planned to proceed from an academic ...spective as the history of Tekong Island is worth exploring. However, ...as worried that the residents had left for Singapore, for the island was ...mandeered for military purposes in 1987. I was also concerned that there ...ght be not enough relevant information and that it might be difficult to ...tact the former residents to obtain the oral history of the Tekong Island. ...nce, I got in touch with my classmate, Lee Hui Ling (李慧玲), and told ...about my research. She thought that this topic was worthy of reporting ...l published details of this project in *Lianhe Zaobao* newspaper on 12 July ...07. On the same day, Mr. Chen and I received numerous calls from the ...mer residents of Tekong Island. When these callers enthusiastically offered ...ir help in the research, my excitement increased and thus I became more ...fident of reconstructing the history of Tekong Island.

During the process of the investigation, the support and encouragement ...m the residents of Tekong Island were my source of momentum for the ...earch. When I plunged into the world of Tekong Island, I realized that ...former residents still missed their homeland; and when I understood the ...ep relationship between the residents and the island, I knew I had to bring ...ir story to the public. I would like to present this book to all the residents ...Tekong Island. This book could not have been completed without your ...luntary information and support, and the story would not be marvelous ...d touching without the life experiences you shared during the research ...ocess.

My thanks go to many friends who helped in this research, including ...s. Lye Soon Choon (赖素春), who voluntarily contacted me and provided

precious information from the archives, Mr. Ho Kim Fong (何金煌) a
Mr. Lea Guan Chong (吕玩俊), who cared about this project and was
great help in acquiring related data. I also appreciate the support fro
Mr. Chen Ting Zhong (陈廷钟) and Ms. Lee Li Chin (李丽珍), who assist
me in interviewing the residents of Tekong Island without any financ
remuneration. My gratitude also goes to Lee Tong Soon (吕同顺), w
sponsored the first meeting of the residents (more than 200 people) so th
we could keep in touch with them for conducting oral interviews. In shor
this project would not have been completed without your help in every ste
I am thankful to Ms. Sun Mei Qiu (孙美球) and Ms. Zhang Lai Ying (张莱丮
of the library of National University of Singapore, who assisted me in writir
the book.

Last but not the least, I want to express my thanks to my famil
With my parents' wholehearted support, I am free to pursue my interest
My beloved wife, Su Ling (淑玲), has been supporting and encouraging n
during the process of my writing the book. During the process of this book
publication, a new member of my family, Jin Gang (劲钢), came into th
world, which is a wonderful icing on the cake. The selfless love of my famil
is the power that pushes me forward, so I love you all. During the time whe
I worked hard in Singapore, Taiwan and Malaysia, I did not feel tired bu
basked in the warmth of my beloved family. I hope I can keep progressin
with love by my side.

Contents

principal investigators of the Research Project on Tekong Island: Chen Poh Seng t) and Lee Leong Sze (Right).

food restaurant and coffee and tea shop at the left side of wharf of Kampong Salabin.

The youth usually camped out nearby the villa at the Permatang.

The welcoming ceremony of the Tuan by temple hosts and director of Chaozho Association at the Sejahat Island had not ceased until reclamation project in 1999.

The residents of Tekong Island draw water from a well Da Jing Tou(大井头).

e water well at Kampong Selabin still existed when the authors arrived at Tekong Island
2008.

Hot spring of Unum in the past.

Hot spring of Unum at present.

CHAPTER 1

Introduction

the largest outlying island of Singapore, Tekong Island[1] (Pulau Tekong) ocated in the northeastern waters of Singapore and functions as an ortant artery of the Johor River. Legend has it that the island had been abited by humans for more than four centuries. Since there is a dearth of orical data, this legend cannot be confirmed. According to the historical a and oral interviews available at present, Malays were dwelling on the nd as early as the mid-19th century. Later, people from southern China migrated to Tekong Island.[2] This outlying island had a population of and 5,000. Along with Singapore, Tekong Island had experienced many iificant events such as the migration of Malays, Chinese and Indians, the asion of Japanese during World War II and regaining of self-governance n the British by the People's Action Party. It also witnessed Singapore's on with the Federation of Malaysia and the former's independence on ugust 1965.

After 1965, Singapore developed rapidly and hence Tekong Island gradly declined, similar to other villages in other highly developed nations. e rapid growth of Singapore attracted the Tekong Island youth, and only elderly and children were left on the island. Adjusting to the trend of velopment, parts of the forest area on Tekong Island were commandeered the government for military purposes in the early 1970s. When Prime nister Lee Kuan Yew visited Tekong Island, he proclaimed that the island uld be developed as a military or industry base within 10 to 12 years and ggested that the residents move to Singapore for a better life.[3]

---

ere was a little island named Pulau Tekong Kechil, inhabited by more than 20 households, luding Chinese and Malays. After Pulau Tekong Kechil was reclaimed by its owner, the residents ved to Tekong Island. In the early times, the Chinese called Tekong Island "Fuluo Beijiang" 罗北降) "Tekuang" or "Beijiang" (北降) in short. *Oral History Interview with Loo Geuang au* (吕玩标) (2007). Singapore: Tekong Island Project; *Oral History Interview with Lea Guan ong* (吕玩俊) (2007). Singapore: Tekong Island Project.

ral *History Interview with Jemaat bin Awang* (1984). Singapore: Oral History Department; l *History Interview with Jaffar bin Kassim* (耶亚华) (2008). Singapore: Tekong Island ject.

tir (《行动报》) (Singapore: People's Action Party Central Committee, 1972).

Under the arrangement of the government, the residents on Tekon Island began migrating in groups to Singapore in the 1970s. The developme of villages on the island ceased as the last group of residents left in 198 Although a remote and backward region, Tekong Island's history still belon to a part of that of Singapore. Some residents from the island achieved gre success in Singapore. Therefore, it is worthwhile to probe into the history Tekong Island. However, it is a pity that this small island, with a populatic of several thousands of people, has been forgotten since all the residen had moved out by 1987. Even former residents had vague memories of t island, which might be an obstacle to research. So far there are only fo publications regarding Tekong Island. The first publication is *Populatic and Usage of Land on Tekong Island* (《德光岛的人口与土地利用》), a thesis bachelor's degree with honors at Nanyang University written by Wu Zhor Bo (吴中博) in 1971. This research investigates Tekong Island's developmen density, distribution, growth, movement, genders and age structure c population, land available for farming, villages and utilization and so c from a geographical perspective. The second publication is *History Pulc Tekong & Tian Kong Buddhist Temple* (《话史德光岛与天降佛堂太阳公庙 written by Ho Kim Fong (何金煌) and published in Singapore in 1993. Th third one is *Loved Tekong* (《恋念德港情》) written by Chong Han (崇汉) an published by Changwu Publishing in Singapore in 1992. Both *History Pulc Tekong & Tian Kong Buddhist Temple* and *Loved Tekong* were writte by former residents of Tekong Island. It can be seen that the author had deep affection for the island. Ho Kim Fong recorded Tekong Island development in the 20th century (including the migration in 1980s) base on his memory. His book also touched upon the distribution of shops o the island, residents' lives and their social interactions. There are also man invaluable photographs of Tekong Island in the book.[4] On the other hand Chong Han wrote about his memories of Tekong in a more literary style The fourth publication is Tan Kim Keong's (陈金强) thesis of bachelor' degree of Department of Chinese Studies with Honors in National Universit of Singapore in 2008, *Opera and Society: Chinese Opera in Singapore a an Example* (《戏剧与社群:以新加坡华族戏曲为例》). Chapter 3 of the thesi explores the history of Tekong Island, the belief of Tuan, opera culture and Chinese identity from the perspective of opera. Since Tekong Islanc is one of the four cases discussed in this thesis, the focus would be placec

---

[4]Photographs in the book depicted shops in Kampong Selabin in 1980s, the streets, the harbor the Malay villages, the church and the Tuan Temple (福音堂;缎伯公庙) and the community center etc.

he belief of Tuan, the culture of opera and relationships in the Chinese
ety.

To sum up, even though there are few publications about Tekong Island,
give us some clues and inspiration for the research. Since so far few
archers have conducted their study on Tekong Island, many potential
arch areas such as ethnic relationships, the development of the village and
influence of Singapore's politics on Tekong Island have not been included
ny research. Since the history of Tekong Island still remains unexplored
he research of Singapore's history and there are so many topics worthy of
ussion, we firmly believe that Tekong Island has potential for research.
The reasons we chose Tekong Island as the subject of the study are
following. One of Chen Poh Seng (陈波生) (whose friends and relatives
former residents of Tekong Island) suggested that we choose this topic.
gradually became interested in the history of Tekong Island during the
cess of preparing for our research as Chen provided valuable information.
il now, no research has solely focused on studying Tekong Island's history.
 meaningful for us to investigate this field as we wish to enrich the history
Singapore. Furthermore, there is a great lack of historical data about the
elopment of Tekong Island, and the number of past residents of the island
lso dwindling each passing year. In our point of view, it is necessary to
serve the present data in order to document the history by writing. Last
 not the least, we have acquired much information from many sources
cluding former residents) during the process of collecting data. The former
idents narrated their experience on Tekong Island, which greatly helped
in our study.

Our research is limited to the period between 1940s and 1980s due
availability of only finite historical data. Documents prior to 1940 or
lier had been lost and Tekong Island officially became a military base in
37. The locations chosen in the study were 14 villages: Kampong Selabin,
mpong Permatang, Kampong Pasir Merah, Kampong Unum, Kampong
ngei Belang, Kampong Ayer Samak, Kampong Pasir, Kampong Pengkalan
kau, Kampong San Yong Kong Parit, Kampong San Yong Kong, Kam-
ng Batu Koyok, Kampong Ladang, Kampong Seminei, Kampong Pahang
d the Chia Tong Quah Estate on the island.[5] The Singapore Government
nmandeered the entire Tekong Island in 1980s and all the residents moved
t of the island. Meanwhile, the development of villages ended. Though
kong Island has greatly changed and it has become more difficult to
nduct studies on this field, it turns more challenging. This research is

---

he estate was also called Zhongho Estate (中和园).

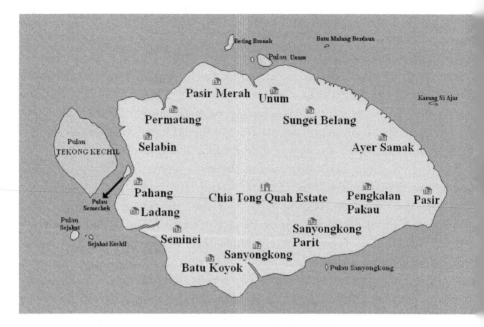

Figure 1.   Distribution of villages on Tekong Island.

conducted without real field work, and the history would be reconstructe
by historical data and oral interviews. Figure 1 shows the distribution o
villages on Tekong Island.

This study focuses on former residents on Tekong Island. Data wer
mainly acquired from four sources: (1) publications related to Tekong Islanc
(2) reports regarding the island's development and residents' activities fror
newspapers and magazines; (3) official documents, recording the educationa
development, community events and census of the island; and (4) ora
interviews with former residents and their descendants and other ora
information obtained from Oral History Department in Singapore.[6]

The research methods in this study can be divided into three types
Literature review prior to the field research is necessary and constructiv
because it helps the research to form a basic structure. After historical data
files, old maps and photographs are collected, their authenticity is confirme
and they are arranged for some clues so that the researcher is able to gai
an initial understanding of the real scenario and human activities. Sinc
the real field no longer exists in case of Tekong Island, documents and file
are more important. This research aims to gather documents, including th
distribution of villages, related historical and geographic data, recording o

---

[6]Singapore Oral History Department once conducted oral interviews with some residents on the
island (including Chinese and Malays) in the 1980s.

y ethnic group, related theories and studies regarding migration, culture arch and ethnography.

The format of an in-depth interview is different from that of a common rview. The purpose of an in-depth interview is to grant the interviewees dom to say anything related to the question in order to gather their ion. It is helpful for the researcher to comprehend and analyze the topic ugh the interviews. Open-response questions are adopted in in-depth rviews to gain more insight into the field of research. In addition to rding the interview, we also observe their facial expressions and body guage because the purpose of the interview is to further analyze the rviewee's way of thinking rather than just record the oral data. Thick ription cannot be achieved without deep understanding. In studying e complicated cultural topics, it is necessary to obtain views from erent people, and cross-interviews are also used to ensure the authenticity vents. In-depth interview provides different aspects for the researcher construct the truth. Based on the researcher's purpose, questions are mulated to acquire open response and offer the interviewees a chance alk about their experiences and memories. This research is expected to ain the former Tekong Island residents' experience of cultural interaction ong different groups, a general picture of how they interacted and Tekong nd's history. In-depth interview works as an important method for field earch to collect data and is complementary to participant observation. e interviewee's experience can be observed through in-depth interview so t the researcher can understand the participant's way of thinking. In this y, there would be a foundation to construct the history.

Suitable for exploration and discovery, participant observation has been e of the significant methods in social studies since the anthropologist nislaw Malinowski adopted this method to study the lives of the residents Trobriand Island. Since human activity is a continuous process and cannot st without real lives, the real meaning is hidden behind the interaction of ly events. Only when the researcher is immersed in the field can people's l lives and the workings of their culture be truly witnessed. By participant servation, we are able to understand the event, related activities, people, 1e, location, the process and its circumstances. Participants' emotions can captured at the moment with a view to thick description. The purpose of rticipant observation is to collect data from the participant's perspective d determine the practical and theoretical truth after analysis. As the l field on Tekong Island disappeared 20 years ago, the former residents 10 moved to Singapore and their lives on Tekong Island are the focus observation. We were once sponsored by the chairman of Thai Village

Holdings, Mr. Lee Tong Soon (吕同顺),[7] to hold a reunion of Tekong Isla:
residents. The attendance was up to 200.[8] During Chinese New Year in 200
we were fortunate to accompany several former residents returning to Teko:
Island, who wanted to relive the environment on the island and the life
that time. We also joined the activities of former Tekong Island residen
that were held in Singapore.[9] We tried to involve ourselves in the residen
lives and obtain their perspective in order to grasp the cultural value a:
meaning of their lives. It is also expected that we can comprehend the proce
of cultural interaction and mergence and further explain the results foun
All these efforts are useful to construct a structure of explanation and tru'
as a combination of theory and knowledge in this research. The followi:
flowchart provides an outline of our study.

This research aims to probe the development and the ethnic relationshi;
of Tekong Island and the influence of Singapore. The history of the isla:
is reconstructed via oral interviews, documents and observation. The deve
opment of villages and the villagers' interactions are also truly recorded :
this study.

The focus of this book is on the development of Tekong Island in rece:
times. Excluding the introduction section of Chapter 1 and conclusion sectic
in Chapter 6, the text is divided into four chapters. In Chapter 2, the shapin
and distribution of villages and way of living of its residents are introduce(
The ethnic structure on Tekong Island is an epitome of that in Singapor(
Therefore, in Chapter 3, the interaction of Chinese and Malays and th
internal relationship within the Chinese is the main focus for the purpos
of understanding the similarity and difference between ethnic groups. A
Tekong Island cannot be separated from Singapore, Chapter 4 investigate
the influence of political events and reform in Singapore and how th
islanders responded to these drastic changes. After independence, Singapor
pitched for modernization, and residents on Tekong Island were forced t
leave their homes. Chapter 5 discusses the reason behind the disappearanc
of villages in Tekong Island and its residents' achievements after moving t
Singapore.

---

[7]Lee Tong Soon was one of the former residents of Kampong San Yong Kong.

[8]The reunion, having the theme "Retrieve Old Memories", was held at Lee's seafood restaurai
in Changi on 22 July 2007. Lianhe Zaobao also sent a journalist to cover the event, and even
was reported in the newspaper the next day. See *Lianhe Zaobao* (《联合早报》) (Singapore) 23 Jul
2007.

[9]The Chaozhouese on Tekong Island established the Chaozhou Corporation (潮州公司) to tak
care of the interests their people and hold prayers during festival from the same hometown. Afte
moving to Singapore, the residents still regularly hold reunions, including dinner twice in a yea
(to celebrate lunar June and the birthday ceremony of Tuan on lunar 15 December).

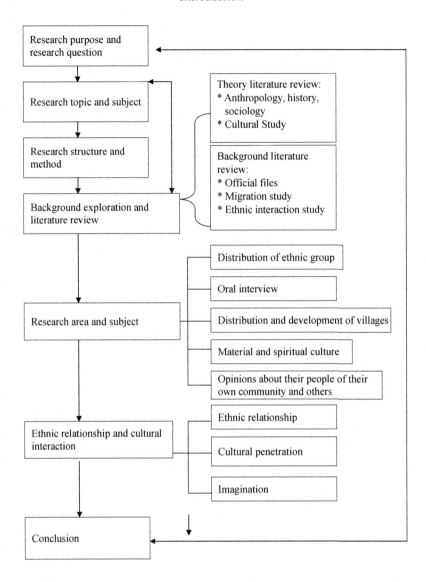

CHAPTER 2

From Desolation to Prosperity

population on Tekong Island mainly comprised migrants from China and Malay Peninsula, making the island a society of immigrants. Migration irs regardless of races and is the result of the interaction of many causes other factors such as the distance of migration and the time of relocation. ed on some scholars' definition of migration, the Taiwanese scholar Liao nghung summarized as follows: (1) migration is the movement from place to another; (2) migration is permanent change of residence; (3) ration may be undertaken by a single person or a group.[1] As to the ation after which migration can be construed as permanent change of dence, Liao proposes that sociologists usually take one, two or five years a criterion for research; a period of five years is usually adopted.[2] From perspective of the above definition to probe into human migration, Malays migrated to Tekong Island more than a century ago and they sidered their migration as moving within their own country. Also, it has been nearly a century since the Chinese migrated overseas to Tekong nd. In terms of the distance, the difference between the Malay and inese relocation is that the former is internal migration and the latter nternational migration.

Migration is caused by the interaction of the "push force" of the country rigin and "pull force" of the destination. "Push force" refers to negative tors, including economic depression, persistent war, weak public security, ural disasters, racial segregation and genocide due to national policy. "Pull ce", on the contrary, is positive appeal, such as a stable and healthy liv-environment, plenty of employment opportunities, good climate, public urity and contact with acquaintances. The idea of "chain migration", as posed by the UN counselor Peter Stalker, emphasizes that acquaintances in destination play a significant role in migration, as observed in the migration Malays and Chinese on Tekong Island. For instance, the Malays on the island inly came from Pahang and Terengganu, whereas the Chinese are mostly kka and Chaozhouese, which correlated with the contact network between

---

ao, C-H (廖正宏) (1985). *Migration.* p. 3. Taipei: San Min Book Co Ltd.
ao, C-H (1985). *Migration* p. 4. Taipei: San Min Book Co Ltd.

migrants. As acquaintances help migrants find a place and a way of living contact network gradually forms under such circumstances.[3]

"Push and pull force" explains the circumstances of migration and t migrant's motivation and need. Every migration consists of choices one aft another: the migrant's choice of migrating or not, the way to migrate a the destination. Stalker maintains that there are two broad approaches: t "individual" and the "structural". The "individual" approach regards ea migrant as a rational human being who carefully selects the best destinatio From the "structural" perspective, the migrant's fate is determined by son force that he cannot control, such as the society and the economy. These tv approaches cannot help in distinguishing their impact on migration althou they help in our understanding of the reasons behind migration.[4] Migratic corresponds to "push and pull force" and involves many issues, includir the circumstances and the migrant's motivation and need.

The agenda of the migrant can be derived from "push and pull force" migration since migration is always related to the individual's free choice. the geographic research of the British and American migration after 1980 the migrant's experience is gradually emphasized on the studying of migratic based on the statistics of large-scale migration, especially refugees, races minority and some specific races. The individual's experience and life would I highlighted to explore migration.[5] This chapter investigates the migration two races by studying the development at that time instead of the individual story of migration. On the other hand, the timeline of the migration of differer races to Tekong Island, the scale of their villages, the way of living and th existence of other institutions, such as religious places, associations, schoo and medical institutes, are also introduced in this chapter.

2.1. Development of Villages

2.1.1. *Migration of the Malays*

According to the archives, it was around 1857 when the Malays migrated t the island. In 1857, the Ruler of Pahang,[6] Tun Ali, passed away, and his son

---

[3]Stalker, P (2001). *The No-Nonsense Guide to International Migration.* p. 24. UK: New Interna tional Publication Ltd.

[4]Stalker, P (2001). *The No-Nonsense Guide to International Migration.* pp. 21–24. UK: Nev International Publication Ltd.

[5]Song, YL (宋郁玲) (2006). Beyond the discipline and transition of migration studies in huma geography: A comparison between Taiwanese anglophonic studies, *Journal of Geographical Science* **43**, p. 67.

[6]Pahang is situated in the east of Malay Peninsula and is the biggest state after Malaysia' independence.

Mutahir succeeded the crown. Tun Mutahir did not follow his father's of granting tax income of Kuantan and Endau[7] to his younger brother ı Ahmad. Wan Ahmad resented Tun Mutahir and, along with his soldiers, ed to Tekong Island, planning his attack in 1857. Wan Ahmad recruited army on the island and prepared to overthrow his brother's regime.[8] In ember 1857, Wan Ahmad attacked and gained preliminary victory with assistance of Sultan Umar of Terengganu. Because trade in Singapore Malay Peninsula was greatly affected due to the civil war in Pahang, governor-general of Singapore went to Pahang, urging for cessation of war. However, as soon as the governor-general left Pahang, Wan Ahmad acked, but returned in vain because of Tun Mutahir's resistance.[9] In March 1861, Wan Ahmad again attacked, in which his small band of iers fought against Tun Mutahir's huge army and emerged victorious. ing high on the success, Wan Ahmad ventured deep into the state of antan in the May 1861, and this time the war lasted for three months. ı Mutahir' General, Mansu, defeated Wan Ahmad's army and the war not end until 1863 when Tun Mutahir and his son Wan Koris passed ιy in succession.[10] On 10 June 1863, Wan Ahmad eventually acquired the wn with the support of chiefs in Pahang.

The six-year civil war had destroyed Pahang, which forced some of its dents to move to Tekong Island by boat and establish their families ıg the coast in southwestern parts of the island. The Malays from Malay ıinsula mainly came from Pahang and few came from Terengganu.[11] The lays named their village Kampong Pahang in memory of their hometown Malay Peninsula.

From 1891 to 1895, a conflict occurred again between the British bassador and chiefs in Pahang. On one hand, the Malay chiefs would accept the regulations put forth by the ambassador and on the other ıd, the Malays were dissatisfied with the ambassador's intervention in hang's politics. The Malays prepared to fight against the British in the l of 1891, and it was not until 1895 that the conflict ceased.[12] The war ıin forced the Malays in Pahang move to Tekong Island. Some of them ¿d in Kampong Pahang and others made the living in other areas on the ınd, establishing Kampong Pasir and Kampong Batu Koyok. In addition

---

present, Kuantan is the capital of Pahang. Endau is governed in the state of Johor.
n Adil HB (1972). *Sejarah Pahang.* p. 119. Kuala Lumpur: Dewan Bahasa dan Pustaka.
n Adil HB (1972). *Sejarah Pahang.* pp. 122–129. Kuala Lumpur: Dewan Bahasa dan Pustaka.
 in Adil HB (1972). *Sejarah Pahang.* pp. 132–133. Kuala Lumpur: Dewan Bahasa dan Pustaka.
)ral *History Interview with Jemaat bin Awang* (1984). Singapore: Oral History Department;
ıl *History Interview with Abu Samah bin Awang* (1987). Singapore: Oral History Department.
in Adil HB (1972). *Sejarah Pahang.* pp. 257–261. Kuala Lumpur: Dewan Bahasa dan Pustaka.

to the information in archives, the names of villages can prove that Mala
were the first group living on Tekong Island, for over half of 14 villag
have Malay names, such as Kampong Pasir Merah, Kampong Permatar
Kampong Sungei Belang, Kampong Ayer Samak, Kampong Pasir, Kampo
Pengkalan Pakau, Kampong Batu Koyok, Kampong Ladang, Kampo
Pahang, Kampong Selabin, etc.[13] All these evidences justify the fact th
the Malays first established villages on Tekong Island.

2.1.2. *Migration of Chinese*

Besides the Malays, Chinese were one of races living on the island a
their migration was related to the situation of China at that time. T
entire Chinese society had changed drastically due to the impact of fle
and cannon from western countries since the first half of the 19th centur
Furthermore, the population in China increased rapidly during the peacef
period of Kangxi Emperor, Yongzheng Emperor and Qianlong Emper
(康熙 雍正 乾隆) in Qing Dynasty (清朝). Nevertheless, the Qing Dynasty h
closed itself from international intercourse for a long time and therefo
its internal productivity was left far behind western countries. The hu
population did not result in high productivity, rather it placed an increasir
strain on the country's resources, which was also competing with Wester
capital and skills. The Qing Dynasty was burdened with a deterioratin
rural economy and increasing population, and its people struggled to ma
a living. Guangdong Province was one of regions facing a huge populatio
stress as it had mountainous terrain with little farmland. Residents c
Guangdong made their living by agriculture, but an increasing number c
people could no longer rely on it. Leaving their hometowns to seek a ne
livelihood seemed to be the only choice.

Possessing the advantage of marine resources, the British were involve
in colonial exploitation in 19th century. They expanded their power to th
Orient and constituted the East India Company, whose principal target wa
to trade with China. For a long time, Malacca Straits had been an importan
channel between China and India. At that time, Malacca and Java wer
occupied by Netherlands, which made it easy for the country to contro
the straits. The British occupied Penang, Sumatra and Bencoolen, whic
lay on the northern part of Malacca Straits and were not ideal places t
command as Penang was too far up north and Bencoolen was not within th

---

[13]"Kampong Pasir Merah" means "village of red sands" in Malay. "Kampong Permatang" refer
to "little village of sand dune". "Kampong Selabin" is the name of a Malay; other villages i
Malaysia were named after the states, landform, names or functions. For example, "Kampon
Pahang" is the name of a state in eastern coast of Malay Peninsula.

route. Therefore, acquiring a stronghold in course of Malacca Straits was priority of the British.

Singapore Island, between China and India, became the British's first rnative as it was an ideal location for controlling Malacca Straits, en-ng the supply of necessities and maintenance of its merchant vessels to na. Furthermore, the location also provided the opportunity to trade Malaya, Indonesia and Indochina Peninsula, so Singapore was able to sform into a trade center between China and Southeast Asia and became rategic geographical post for transit trade.

The above incentives encouraged East India Company to set up a iness center in Singapore; thus the Bencoolen Deputy Governor-General mas Stamford Raffles was assigned to prospect Singapore. When Raffles led on this island on 29 January 1819, it was nothing more than a little ing village with only 150 residents (30 of them were Chinese). With a v of realizing East India Company's plan, Raffles concluded an agreement 30 January with Temenggong Abdul Rahman to develop Singapore as a ish trading post and settlement. On 6 February, Raffles signed a treaty h Sultan Hussein,[14] and East India Company officially rented Singapore, sessing a significant location within Malacca Straits.

The year 1824 was important, when Great Britain and Netherlands, on March, reached an agreement in which the two countries demarcated their pe. The British abdicated East Indies and Bencoolen, while the Dutch e up Malaya. Thus, the British laid a solid foundation for expanding its ver and started colonial rule in Malaya. Since then, the British spared effort in developing Malaya and Singapore. At that time, insufficient nan resources hampered development, and introduction of foreign labor s necessary. China, with a large population, was the primary target of British.[15] China was facing internal social unrest and external invasion m western countries. Besides, corruption in the Qing Dynasty and the rsening plight of people made migration the only choice of survival.

Before 1876, there were at least six agencies in China's trading posts ering workforce for Singapore, including foreign firms operated by busi-ssmen, Ho's (合记), Yuan Xing's Store (元兴行) and Di Chang (地常) run Chinese. The first two stores were located in Shantou and the last one in noy.[16] Chinese who migrated to Singapore consisted of contract laborers d many migrants introduced by their relatives or fellow townsmen, such

t that time, Singapore was the territory of Johor.

hiang, HD (1978). *A History of Straits Settlements Foreign Trade 1870–1915*. pp. 8–9. gapore: National Museum.

Vang, XW (王省吾) (1978). *Chinese's Migration Agencies 1848–1888*. pp. 355–360. San ncisco: Chinese Information Center.

as wives, sons, daughters, brothers and other members in the family w
founded a company overseas and needed employees. These Chinese main
came from coastal provinces in southern China, composed of Cantone$
Hakka, Fujianese, Chaozhouese and migrants from Hainan. To encoura
Tekong Island's development, the colonial government claimed that anyo
willing to cultivate land on the island could own the land.[17] The policy dr$
many Chinese, who planted gambir and pepper. The explorers also recruit$
contract labor to work on Tekong Island for a term of three to five years.

It was in early 20th century when the Chinese population rockete
The colonial government had begun to cultivate rubber because of its hi$
demand and appealing price, and Tekong Island, with its huge swathes
space for cultivation, was appropriate for the growth. A Chinese Musli
Ishak[19] arrived on Tekong Island from Terengganu and started the grow
of rubber in awareness of its value. He earned a fortune because of the risi$
price of rubber and then expanded the business and was followed by oth$
people into this field. The rubber plantations on Tekong Island therefo
developed rapidly and led to the need for more workforce. The Chine$
migrated to the island at this juncture. Thus the population increase
sharply, resulting in the change of the composition of races on the island. Th
Chinese established their villages, such as Kampong Sanyongkong Parit,
Kampong Sanyongkong and Chia Tong Quah Estate.

The colonial government aggressively developed Malaya by introducin
Chinese and Indian workers as well. There were less than 20 Indians[21] livin
on Tekong Island according to the statistics between 1957 and 1969; henc$
Indians would not be discussed in the text. In the following sections, th

---

[17]The colonial government divided the term of land ownership into three: 30, 99 and 999 year
Wu, ZB (1971). *Population and Usage of Land on Tekong Island.* pp. 4–5. Unpublished hono:
thesis, Nanyang University.
[18]*Oral History Interview with Ng Kia Chew* (黄镜秋) (1982). Singapore: Oral History Departmen
[19]According to Ho Kim Fong's record, the name of the Chinese Muslim was Liang Sanho (梁三合
(from Hainan), who lived in Kampong Pahang and was also the first village head; Ho, KF (1987
History Pulau Tekong & Tian Kong Buddhist Temple. p. 11. Singapore: Ho, KF; *Oral Histor*
Interview with Chin Sit Har (陈锡霞) (1987). Singapore: Oral History Department.
[20]This village was also called "Under Pigpen" (豬寮下) because there had been only one woma
living in this village and she made the living by pig farming. In another version, Hakka was engage
in pig farming so they called the village "Under Pigpen." *Oral History Interview with Antung L$
(李安东) (2007). Singapore: Tekong Island Project; *Oral History Interview with Ng Kia Che$
(1982). Singapore: Oral History Department.
[21]The census in 1957 showed that there were 44 Indian and Pakistani descendants. In the surve
conducted by Department of Geography of Nanyang University in 1969, there were only 3 India:
descendants; there were 11 Indian descendants according the census in 1980. *Report on the Censu*
of Population 1957 (1964), p. 109. Singapore: Government Printer; Wu, ZB (1971), *Populatio*
and Usage of Land on Tekong Island, p. 8. Unpublished honors thesis, Nanyang University; *Censu*
of Population 1980 Singapore (1981), p. 14. Singapore: Department of Statisitcs.

cture of villages on Tekong Island, the way of living of the residents and facilities available on the island are introduced.

Life in Villages

1. *Structure of village*

ɔng Island served as an important port during the end of 19th century early 20th century. Since at that time the principal mode of trans-tation was sailboats, the boat from Tanjong Sulat and Kota Tinggi to ɡapore berthed at Tekong Island if it encountered stormy waves. The ɔrs sold local products to merchants on the island and purchased daily ɛssities at the same time. People from Changi and Pulau Ubin (Ubin nd) conducted business on Tekong Island, and it was a major trade center ween Changi Johor (see Fig. 2).[22] Resident Ng Kia Chew once indicated

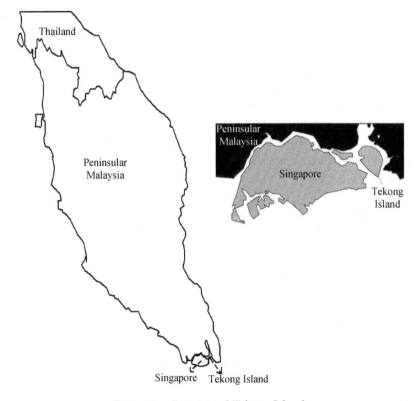

Figure 2. Position of Tekong Island.

Ɉral History Department (1990), *Recollection: People and Places*, p. 62. Singapore: Oral tory Department; Wu, ZB (1971). *Population and Usage of Land on Tekong Island*, p. 5. published honors thesis, Nanyang University.

Boss of Lian Sheng Grocery Store and his wife (right) were purchasing bananas harve
offered by villagers.

the importance of Tekong Island: "it (Tekong Island) had been an exist. A
sailboats going either south or north came here as the roads in the harbor
Malaya were obstructed. Later, ships also had to pass through this post.
Changi did not lead to town (the commercial area now). There was no roa
or passage that led there. Residents in Pulau Ubin also bought commoditi
on Tekong Island. People from Johore, in Tanjung Surat, even in Kota Ting
purchased on this island."[23] Tekong Island thrived with the development c
trade by its ideal geographical position, which transformed Kampong Selabi
on the island into a commercial center. From the survey in the early 1970s
among 62 stores on the island, 45 were in Kampong Selabin[24] and they wer
grocery stores, coffee shops, restaurants, general stores, Chinese Medical Ha
and pork stores. There were only grocery stores in other villages, excep
for Kampong Sanyongkong Parit, which had a coffee shop. All stores o
Tekong Island were owned by the Chinese, except two.[25] Kampong Selabi
was the only alternative for residents in other villages for the purchase o
daily necessities, which made Kampong Selabin the commercial center of th
island. From the picture, it can be observed that Tekong Island was locate

---

[23] *Oral History Interview with Ng Kia Chew* (1982). Singapore: Oral History Department.
[24] Wu, ZB (1971). *Population and Usage of Land on Tekong Island*, p. 42. Unpublished honor
thesis, Nanyang University.
[25] One of the two stores was operated by a Malayan and the other was run by an Indian. Wu, Zl
(1971). *Population and Usage of Land on Tekong Island*, Unpublished honors thesis, p. 44
Nanyang University.

near the river mouth and Kampong Selabin was in the western side of
island. Boats had to pass through Kampong Selabin, which transformed
a commercial hub.

Kampong Pahang was the administrative center of the island and its
ghulu (head of village) was also from the village like the first Penghulu
.k, second Penghulu Tengku Ahmad bin Tengku Sulong and the third
ghulu Jemaat bin Awang. The villagers mainly worked in administrative
itute or in Changi, which was different from that of other villages. Fishing
.ges existed, and agriculture was also practiced in some villages on the
.d. Fishing villages consisted of Kampong Permatang, Kampong Pasir
'ah, Kampong Seminei, Kampong Pasir, Kampong Ladang and Kampong
'r Samak; and agricultural villages included Kampong Sungei Belang,
npong Pengkalan Pakau, Kampong Sanyongkong Parit, Kampong Sany-
kong, Kampong Batu Koyok and the Chia Tong Quah Estate.

.2. *Life on Tekong Island*

ould be seen from the structure of villages that residents on the island
e mainly engaged in fishery and agriculture. Crops included rubber,
etables, tobacco and coconuts. As for commercial activities, there were
:es on the island in charge of buying crops from farmers. For instance,
.ng Ge Bao (黄歌保) from Chaozhou operated Shun Cheng Store (顺成号),
ing grocery, and buying vegetable and fruits and reselling them to
gapore. In another business, coconut[26] was processed, dried and sold
Singapore.[27] The Hakka Chen Bing-kui (陈炳奎) ran his grocery store
.ang Fa Xing (广发兴), carrying local products by boat to Singapore and
.ing them; he also brought back foreign products and sold them on the
.nd.[28] After World War II, merchants on Tekong Island tried to expand
ir business outward like Hakka Xie Yumin (谢裕民) and Xie Fu (谢浮),
o invested in Yu Yuan Store (裕源商行) for cloth import and export.[29]

There were not many businessmen on the island, and agriculture was
: principal way of living. Hakka, who accounted for most farmers in
.kong Island, might have tried to replicate their original living environment

)ral History Interview with Ho Lian Ying (何莲英) (2007). Singapore: Tekong Island Project.
.l History Interview with Hong Chu Lan (洪竹兰) (2007). Singapore: Tekong Island Project.
.l History Interview with Guo Hong-Xia (郭红霞) (2007). Singapore: Tekong Island Project.
.l History Interview with Ho Mei Mei (何美妹) (2007). Singapore: Tekong Island Project.
)ral History Interview with Huang Sheng Jie (黄盛杰) (2007). Singapore: Tekong Island Project.
.l History Interview with Ng Swee Chiang (黄瑞章) (2007). Singapore: Tekong Island Project.
)ral History Department (1990). *Recollection: People and Places*, p. 61. Singapore: Oral History
partment.
nformation provided by Ho Kim Fong.

Rubber plantation of Tekong Island.

The authors found piles of red bricks marked TEKONG at the relics of the brickwo: of Tan Kah Kee before World War II.

in China. Hakka on Tekong Island came from Dapu, Chiayingzhou an Fengshun in Guangdong. Many of them had resided inland in Guangdon Province and agriculture was their main source of living. Except for a fe Hakka engaged in business, most Hakka on Tekong Island were farmers, an especially planted rubber. A local leader, Chin Sit Har, once composed Hakka song, mirroring the Hakka's way of living:

> Tapping rubber at five with light. Having breakfast at eight. It's ten after rubber has been made and collecting firewood on the way. Tapping rubber almost complete. It's dusk and cloudy. Rain falls and wind comes, all hard work is in vain. Rain stops harvesting and having rice with water for breakfast. Plucking wild vegetable as no income for rice. Straping waist belt and waiting for tomorrow. Planting banana instead of rubber. Sweet potatoe, taro and vegetable. Everybody works hard together. Money is saved to support the family.[30]

Besides agriculture, some residents, both Chinese and Malays, made thei living by fishing. The Chaozhouese were predominantly involved in fishing[31]

---

[30]Chin, SH (2008). Song of rubber tapper, *Journal of Ying Fo Fui Kun*, **16**, p. 15.
[31]*Oral History Interview with Loo Geuang Fiyau* (2007). Singapore: Tekong Island Project *Oral History Interview with Heng Siew Leng* (王首龙) (2007). Singapore: Tekong Island Project *Singapore Tekong Island Chaozhou Tuan Kong Beo Temple*, p. 2. Singapore: Tuan Kong Be Temple, 1985.

e were also some islanders who worked at the police office and schools
he island.

Prior to World War II, the Singapore businessman Tan Kah Kee[32]
blished a brickwork factory on the island, and another businessman Loo
structed a pottery manufacturing vase and vat.[33] The factories provided
ployment for islanders, and farmers on the island also partly did business
he same time.[34] To sum up, agriculture and fishery were the primary
apations on Tekong Island, and industry, business and public institutes
provided work for islanders.

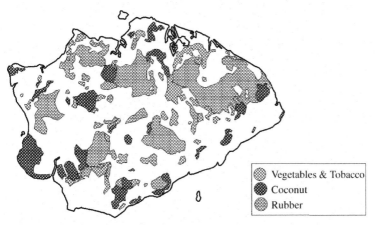

	Vegetables & Tobacco
	Coconut
	Rubber

Land Use Map of Pulau Tekong 1960 based on Wu, ZB (1971)

.3. *Religious places, clan associations, community centers, schools and medical institutes*

.3.1. *Religious places*

e migration of Chinese and Malays in mid-19th century greatly trans-
med the originally desolate Tekong Island, and a vibrant society thus

an Kah Kee (陈嘉庚), born on 21 October 1874 in Jimei (集美), Donguan County (同安),
an Province followed his father for business in Singapore at age of 17 years and succeeded at
of 30 years. Tan's factory was divided into three departments: raw and ripe rubber processing,
ber forest and pineapple farm. His business was expanded to Singapore, Malaysia, Borneo,
na, Indonesia, Myanmar, Thailand, Vietnam and Philippines. Offices were also set in five
tinents. Tan was good at socializing and always funded the development of Chinese education.
contribution to education made him the leader among Chinese in Singapore and Malaysia.
)ral History Interview with Heng Siew Leng (2007). Singapore: Tekong Island Project; Oral
tory Interview with Lea Guan Chong (2007). Singapore: Tekong Island Project.
mall part of stores on the island opened at noon for its owner and his family worked in the
n or reaped rubber in the morning. Wu, ZB, *Population and Usage of Land on Tekong Island*,
20. Unpublished honors thesis, Nanyang University.

Altars at Jiang Fu Temple (also called Three Gods Temple).

Relics of Jiang Fu Temple (also called Three Gods Temple).

gradually developed. Under these circumstances, migrants had to confront the vagaries of nature and compete with other races, which gave rise to the desire for peace and security. Religious places were established to relieve migrants from stress and offer support to them. According to limited information, Malay mosques were present only in Kampong Selabin, Kampong Pasir and Kampong Pahang[35] and hence would not be mentioned in this section. The focus here is on Chinese temples.

---

[35] *Oral History Interview with Abdullab bin Ahmad* (1984). Singapore: Oral History Department.

There were six temples located among villages on Tekong Island. Only 4
ᵔese temples that are older than 50 years are introduced in the text due
◀sufficient information. Jiang Fu Temple (降福宫) (also called Three Gods
▪ple)[36] did not exist physically at first. In the 19th century, the statue of
▪god was carried from China by the Hakka Zhong Shan Ling (钟山灵) to his
▪se on Tekong Island. After Zhong passed away, his son Zhong Yuanyuan
亡运) continued worshipping the god. It was rumored that every time Zhong
nyuan walked to the crossroad of the Chinese Cemetery, strong winds blew
rain fell. Zhong Yuanyuan thus called upon villagers for constructing the
ple, which was named Jiang Fu Temple, and escorted Three Gods from his
▪se to the temple. In 1949, Jiang Fu Temple was renovated and continued to
ᵔess the development of Tekong Island. It did not close until the 1980s when
island was commandeered by the government.[37]

Tianzhao Buddhist Temple (天照佛堂) (also named Guanyin Temple) was
▪mple more than a century old, and its founder Chen Bing Kui (陈炳奎)
▪ the owner of a gambir farm. He carried Guanyin Bodhisattva and Matzu
▪n Mei County of Guangdong Province and worshipped them in a temple
▪is farm. He hence named the temple Tianzhao Buddhist Temple. Gods
▪e still worshipped in Tian Kong Buddhist Temple[38] when the islanders
in 1987. De An Temple (德安宫) in Sanyongkong was another temple on
▪ong Island whose abbot was Chen Ying Chang (陈营昌). During 1940s to
▪0s, huge numbers of pilgrims visited the temple. After the abbot passed
▪y, his descendant was not willing to succeed and migrated to Singapore,
▪ therefore De An Temple was closed accordingly.[39]

The Chinese on Tekong Island held rituals in honor of God of Tuan[40]
every 15 December of the lunar calendar. What made Tuan unique
▪ that there was no statue of the god, but a huge stone on Pulau
▪ahat (Sejahat Island)[41] was worshipped. According to the statements
▪he islanders, Tuan was a Malay general of Aceh Kingdom in the 16th
▪tury. He committed suicide with his soldiers after being defeated by
▪ Portuguese army in a war. In the early 19th century, boats tended to

───────────────

egend has it that three gods refer to god of wind, thunder and rain. Ho, KF (1987). *History Pulau*
▪ong & Tian Kong Buddhist Temple, p. 66. Singapore: Ho, KF.
▪o, KF (1987). *History Pulau Tekong & Tian Kong Buddhist Temple*, pp. 66–67. Singapore:
KF.
▪o, KF (1987). *History Pulau Tekong & Tian Kong Buddhist Temple*, p. 70. Singapore: Ho, KF.
▪formation provided by Chen Ting Zhong (陈廷钟).
▪he Hakka on Tekong Island called God of Tuan "Tuan Kungyeh" while Chaozhouese called it
▪an Kung". From pictures and archives, the god was called Tuan which would be used in the
▪ for consistency.
Pulau Sejahat" means "Island of Evil" in Malay. Iskandar, T (1986). *Kamus Dewan*. p. 430.
▪ala Lumpur: Dewan Bahasa dan Pustakap. Sejahat Island was named Tuan Islet after villagers
▪ted to worship Tuan.

run against rocks when passing through Sejahat Island. At the same tin
villagers of Kampong Selabin found that an elderly Malay man often can
to the village from Sejahat Island by boat and went back after lingeri:
around the village. The appearance of the old man bewildered the village:
who then followed him to Sejahat Island. After arriving on the island, t.
villagers found only a huge stone standing in the middle of the island.
The Chinese started to worship the old man for the safety of residents c
Tekong Island and regarded the stone as the old Malay.[43] Every year,
December on the lunar calendar was also celebrated as the birthday of Tua
Tuan was first placed in Guandong and Fujian Associates and the annu
ritual was held by the hall. Later, the Chaozhouese also organized their ow
association, so the ritual of Tuan was held respectively by two organization
After World War II, the two associations agreed to hold the ritual togethe
Tuan then was worshipped at the Tian Kong Buddhist Temple in Bedo
North after residents left Tekong Island.[44] (see Chapter 3)

2.2.3.2. *Clan associations and community center*

The construction of clan associations was a result of migration. A migrar
who arrived in a new environment is filled with dread and fear at tl
absence of friends or relatives to rely on and the obstacles posed by tl
language barrier. How much a newcomer hoped someone could help to fin
a job and accommodation! Relations and friends became the supportiv
power for migrants in a strange place, so people from the same hometow
tended to live near each other. The Chinese were connected by affectio
of the same homeland and blood relations and the clan seemed to b
a protective umbrella in their subconsciousness.[45] Guangdong & Fujia
Association founded by Chen Bing Kui[46] in the 1890s was also starte
under such circumstances. Situated in Kampong Selabin, the associatio
aimed at developing education and promoting welfare for islanders, and it
founder was elected as the first director.[47] There were activities held b

---

[42]Ho, KF (1987). *History Pulau Tekong & Tian Kong Buddhist Temple*, pp. 42–43. Singapore
Ho, KF.

[43]In 1970s, one of the islanders bought a statue of Dato Kung, placing it on the huge rock c
Sejahat Island and considering it Tuan. *Oral History Interview with Lea Guan Chong* (2007)
Singapore: Tekong Island Project.

[44]Tian Kong Buddhist Temple was constructed by the constructor Liu Lun Chun (刘伦春) i
Kampong Pasir Merah in the spring of 1960s.

[45]Editing Committee of Federation of Clan Association (2005). *20 Years of Federation of Cla*
Association, p. 9. Singapore: Singapore Federation of Chinese Clan Associations.

[46]Chen was the first generation of migrants from Mei County in China. He planted gambir anc
pepper on the island and was quite successful on his business.

[47]*Oral History Interview with Chin Sit Har* (1987). Singapore: Oral History Department.

association, including the ritual of absolution for ghosts on 15 July and celebration for Tuan's birthday on 15 December of the lunar calendar. the latter event was important to the Chinese society on the island, bers of the association collected funds for the activity from residents stores and constructed a stage and temporary shrine on the road.[48] re the celebration began, members of the council escorted Tuan from hat Island by boat and placed it in the temporary shine so that the lents and pilgrims[49] could worship it. Guangdong & Fujian Association ed at the time residents of Tekong Island left in 1987.

In the 1930s, the leaders of Tekong Island from Chaozhou, Huang Ge Bao 保) and Huang Zai Biao (黄再标), took the lead, purchasing land and ding and founded Chaozhou Corporation,[50] which was organized for the pose of connecting and assisting the Chaozhouese. On the other hand, corporation also cooperated with Guangdong & Fujian Association in ling the ceremony to celebrate Tuan's birthday. Before leaving the island, Chaozhouese decided to retain Chaozhou Corporation after several dis- sions and to lead a new life in a new city based upon the spirit of mutual stance. After moving to Singapore, the members decided to formally ster the association. The archives of the association said, "After 9 rs (1985–1994) of studying local laws... we decided to register the ociation."[51] Heads of the corporation believed they should adopt the ne "Tuan Kong Beo Temple" when communicating with government artments. To avoid unnecessary misunderstanding, "Tuan Kong Beo nple" was used to replace "Chaozhou Corporation."[52] The association, ich existed for more than 50 years old on Tekong Island, was officially istered as a society by the Singapore Registry of Societies on 4 July 1994, h its building located in Tian Kong Buddhist Temple. So far more than) members are part of the association and reunions are held twice a year, pectively, in the middle of lunar June and on 25 December, which is also an's birthday.[53] Tuan Kong Beo Temple is one of few associations that tinue to function after its members moved out of Tekong Island; Kuo

ral History Interview with Huang Ming Xuan (黄明轩) (2007). Singapore: Tekong Island ject, 2007; Oral History Interview with Wang Shou Qing (王首清) (2007). Singapore: Tekong nd Project.
1 addition to islanders, residents on Ubin Island and Johor Harbor made pilgrimages to Tuan.
l History Interview with Loo Geuang Fiyau (2007). Singapore: Tekong Island Project.
ral History Interview with Loo Geuang Fiyau (2007). Singapore: Tekong Island Project; Oral tory Interview with Heng Siew Leng (2007). Singapore: Tekong Island Project.
ingapore Tekong Island Chaozhou Tuan Kong Beo Temple, p. 3. Singapore: Tuan Kong Beo nple.
bid.
ral History Interview with Heng Siew Leng (2007). Singapore: Tekong Island Project; Oral tory Interview with Loo Geuang Fiyau (2007). Singapore: Tekong Island Project.

Wu is another clan association [comprised of members whose surname Kuo (郭屋)]. As these people still keep in contact, every year, one fam is in charge of the ritual of commemorating their ancestors. The fam responsible leads everyone to conduct ancestral worship at the Singapo Mandai Memorial Columbaria in the last week of lunar July. They also hi a Taoist priest from Kulai,[54] praying to ancestors, and have a meal togeth after the ritual is completed.[55]

A group photo of members of Pulau Tekong Community Center and head of village Tengk Ahmad bin Tengku Sulong (sixth from right, front row).

Life on Tekong Island was simple; the residents started work at dawn an rested at dusk. In the middle of 1950s, two businessmen from Chaozhou Huang Ruei Zhang (黄瑞璋) and Huang Xi Di (黄细弟), started a join venture of open-air cinema on a vacant land beside the northward road i Kampong Selabin, which became a source of entertainment for the resident of Tekong.[56] After People's Action Party took over the regime in 195? two community centers, Pulau Tekong Community Center in Kampon Pahang and Kampong Selabin Community Center in Kampong Selabin, wei erected in 1963 with a view of providing a place for islanders' entertainmen These two community centers held activities such as kindergarten educatior sewing and embroidery class for women, badminton team, National Da celebrations, sailboat and bike competitions and trips to Singapore fo visiting newspaper offices. Community centers also conduct "welfare week'

---

[54]Kulai is one of counties in the south of Johor.
[55]Information provided by Guo Jin Long (郭金龙).
[56]Ho, KF (1987). *History Pulau Tekong & Tian Kong Buddhist Temple*, p. 103. Singapore: Ho, KF.

"elderly day" in accordance with the tradition in Changi so that people
fferent races are involved in the activities.

3.3. *School*

lese language education in Singapore began in the middle of 19th
ury. At first, schools followed the traditional Chinese education, adopting
fucian treatises, such as Classic of Filial Piety, Great Learning and
trine of the Mean. At the end of 19th century, reformers and revolution-
s went south to Singapore, propagating their own ideas and constructing
lernized schools. Under their influence, schools were established in the
western countries did, in lieu of the old-style private schools. The
rmed Chinese education still followed the educational system in China:
years of primary school, three years in junior high school and three years
enior high school. The curriculum was also the same as that in China
extbooks were from publishers in China, Zhunghua Book Company and
Commercial Press; also, most teachers came from China.[57] Students
e deeply influenced by China in "transplanted education",[58] for they
e concerned about China and familiar with its geography and history.
colonial government was aware of the impact of development of Chinese
cation on their reign. Accordingly, it altered its policy on free develop-
t of Chinese education and issued the Registration of Schools Ordinance,
which any school with more than ten students had to register with the
ernment authority. The government had right to revoke its registration[59]
he school was found disturbing the peace of the community. Regardless of
ernment's surveillance, Chinese education still expanded and developed
h the people's support and their respect of their culture and education.

The Chinese educational system on Tekong Island was similar to that in
gapore. There was a total of six Chinese schools on the island in various
iods (one was public and five were private), and four of them were in
mpong Sanyongkong: Chong Fah School (中华学校) founded by Chen Bo
ng (陈伯堂), Aik Fah School (益华学校) founded by Xie Yu Xi (谢玉溪)

ʃang, GW (王赓武) (2002). Chinese Overseas: the Past in the Future. In *New Research
ections on the Chinese Overseas*, Liu, H (刘宏) and Huang, JL (黄坚立) (eds.), pp. 39–40.
A: Global Publishing; Choi, KK (崔贵强) (1990). *Recognition and Transformation of Singapore
Malaysia*, pp. 19–20. Singapore: Singapore Nanyang Association.
he development of the school was based upon the sound system of the school and instructions
n China. Doraisamy, TR (1969). *150 Years of Education in Singapore*, p. 78. Singapore:
chers' Training College.
Ioraisamy, TR (1969). *150 Years of Education in Singapore*, pp. 86–87. Singapore: Teachers'
ining College.

in 1931, Chung Foh School (中和学校) founded by Guo Zi Yi (郭子翼)
who was also the principal and Cheng Kong School (正光学校) founded
the Principal Chen Ran Qiu (陈染秋) in the 1950s. The other two schoo
were located in Kampong Selabin[61]: Eng Wah School (英华学校) found
by Yang Yong Chang (杨永昌) and Oi Wah School (爱华学校). The latt
had been a private school started by the Chinese leader Chen Bing Kui
1886 and gratuitously offered the chance of education for Chinese childre
In 1920s, the school no longer attracted increasing number of students, a
a new educational system from China was introduced. Chen Bing Kui,
the director of Guangdong & Fujian Association, led local stores and folks
erect new buildings of the school and named it "Oi Wah School"(爱华学校).
After World War II, Oi Wah School transformed as a public school and w
merged into the Pulau Tekong Integrated School by the government in 196

Folk dance performed by students of Pulau Tekong Integrated School on occasion
Athletic Games in 1963.

Chinese was the main language of instruction in Chinese schools o
Tekong Island. There was one exception: Aik Fah School founded by th
principal and teacher, Xie Yu Xi (谢玉溪), adopted Hakka as its language c
instruction in 1950s. At its peak, there were more than 40 students.[63] Ther
were six Chinese schools on Tekong Island, and each developed differentl

[60]*Oral History Interview with Lai Wan Qing* (赖万清) (2007). Singapore: Tekong Island Project
[61]Most residents in Kampong Selabin were Chinese. The Chaozhouese called the place "Gan,
Jiao" (港脚) and Hakka called it "Gang Xia"(港下).
[62]*Pulau Tekong School file.* Singapore: National Archives of Singapore. Ref: ME 3877.
[63]*Oral History Interview with Antung Lee* (2007). Singapore: Tekong Island Project. Informatio
provided by Chen Ting Zhong (陈廷钟).

Wah School was merged into Oi Wah School in 1954; Aik Fah School
:d in 1960s when the buildings of Cheng Kong School (正光学校) were
it down, so its temporary schoolhouses were borrowed from Chung Foh
)ol. At that time, the principal of Chung Foh School, Guo Zi Yi, was
it to retire so the boards of two school decided to amalgamate Chung
   School with Cheng Kong School and named it Chung Kong
)ol.[64] The principal of Cheng Kong School, Chen Ran Qiu, took the
; of the new principal of Chung Kong School in which there were four
·hers.[65] On 1 January 1967, the board agreed to close Chung Kong School
to difficulty in enrolling new students and management.[66]

To raise the quality of education, the government constructed Pulau
ong School in Kampong Pahang in the late 1950s. The Ministry of
ication divided this primary school into two sections: Pulau Tekong
;lish School and Pulau Tekong Chinese School (Oi Wah School) on 11
uary 1960. On 21 January, the ministry ceased the registration of Oi
h School and two schools, respectively, used seven classrooms of the
)olhouse. The English school was operated based on related ordinances,
:reas the Chinese school was subsidized by the government. The English
)ol's principal was responsible for the management of the schoolhouse
: the facility provided by the government while the other Chinese school's
icipal was in charge of equipment borrowed from other departments. The
nber of students, according to the statistics of the ministry in 1961, was
   in the Chinese school and 201[67] in the English school. The Ministry of
ication officially merged the two schools (still divided into Chinese and
;lish sections) after a year and assigned one principal to the school, mod-
ng the name from "Pulau Tekong School" to "Pulau Tekong Integrated
1ool." [The penultimate principal was Mr. Chen Shiao Chern (陈绍深)]

Besides Chinese and English schools, there were also Pulau Tekong Malay
iool and Kampong Pasir Malay School for Malay children. Based on the
tistics from Ministry of Education in 1959, there were 83 students (six
.des) in Pulau Tekong Malay School.[68] Kampong Pasir Malay School shut
vn in the 1970s as the Ministry of National Defense commandeered the

ral History Interview with Lai Wan Qing (2007). Singapore: Tekong Island Project; informa-
 : provided by Chen Ting Zhong.
 here were three Chinese teachers, Lo Yong Cong (罗永琮), Cheng Shao Kui (程少葵), Chen
 Yun (陈丽云) and one English teacher, Chen Shi Min (陈世民). Information provided by Chen
 g Zhong.
'hung Kwang School file 27 March 1967. Singapore: National Archives of Singapore. Ref: ME
 4.
'ulau Tekong School file. Singapore: National Archives of Singapore. Ref. ME 3877.
'ulau Tekong Malay School file. Singapore: National Archives of Singapore. Ref: ME 3864.

Kampong Pasir Malay School buildings.

Deserted school.

land.[69] The education of language on Tekong Island was limited to primar
school level, so students had to pursue further studies in Singapore.

2.2.3.4. *Medical institute*

Because of its location near the border, medical institutions on Tekong Islan
were simple and basic. Due to the lack of hygienic conditions and tap water

---

[69]The site of the school is preserved quite well.

Dormitory of an employee of the clinic in Kampong Pahang.

pail for stool required everyday cleaning. The only source of drinking
er was the well.[70] According to the records of an employee, George T
les, hired by English soldiers, medical institutions did not exist[71] on
ong Island until the late 1950s, when the government set up a clinic
Kampong Pahang. The clinic provided simple medical service, infant
k powder, vitamin, butter and so on. A doctor and a nurse came weekly
n Singapore to examine pregnant women.[72] Resident Chen Chun Rong
春蓉) recollected that in the 1940s, there was a nurse called Ms. Yang Ya
(杨亚发) who was enthusiastic about serving the villagers. Yang spared no
rt even though she had to help a woman deliver a child in the midnight,
which the residents felt grateful.[73] In 1968, Dr. Yap Kok Keng and
other doctor opened a private clinic in joint venture and they had operated
clinic until 1978, when it was closed down due to poor performance.[74] In
'8, Dr. Lim Hock Siew (林福寿) was brought to Tekong Island by Internal
urity Department after 15 years of detainment as he was arrested in 1963
his identity as a committeeman of Barisan. Lim was a political prisoner
l also the only doctor[75] on the island. He was allowed to move freely, work
l live with his family but could not leave the island without permission.
e government planned to hire Dr. Lim as a replacement of Dr. Yap, but

ral History Interview with Yap Kok Keng (DR.) (1999). Singapore: Oral History Department.
ral History Interview with George T James (1984). Singapore: Oral History Department.
ral History Interview with Sia Seng Lan (2000). Singapore: Oral History Department.
ral History Interview with Chen Chun Rong (陈春蓉) (2007). Singapore: Tekong Island Project.
ral History Interview with Yap Kok Keng (DR.) (1999). Singapore: Oral History Department.
ianhe Zaobao (Singapore), 9 September 2007.

he refused. However, Dr. Lim still saw patients for free and the villagers we
thus grateful for his behavior. Dr. Lim recalled, "Villagers were very friend
They gave me food for free, including vegetables they planted and fish th
caught by themselves. What I ate the most was durian. It was on Teko
Island that I ate the most durian."[76] Lim was released on 6 September 19
and went back to Singapore. Regardless of the 19-year detainment, the
years on Tekong Island was Lim's most memorable life.

Religious institutions and associations were places of comfort and pea
for the residents, while community centers, schools and medical institut
were important places for development of the society on the island. Despi
its remote location and lack of tall buildings and modernized facilitie
residents on the island still led their lives in a peaceful way.

2.3. Conclusion

Located to the northeast of Singapore, Tekong Island was once a fortifie
position in southern Johor and also a base of counterattack in the civil wi
of Pahang. Due to the chaos caused by the war in Malay Peninsula, son
Malays migrated to Tekong Island and constructed their residences, formir
villages one by one. On the other hand, internal revolt and external invasic
in China encouraged Chinese' migration to Tekong Island and most of the
were Hakka, who also erected their own dwellings and hence formed sever
large villages. The migration of Malays and Chinese led to the prosperit
of Tekong Island. The Malays made their living mainly by fishing, whi
the Chinese planted rubber, coconut and tobacco besides being involved i
fishing. The Chinese also knew how to conduct business; therefore, ther
were markets and stores in Chinese villages like Kampong Selabin and
brickwork factory was constructed. These commercial activities stimulate
the economy and job market on Tekong Island.

Migration is one of the elements for human progress, so are religion an
folk beliefs. In Tekong Island, Chinese temples and Malay mosques wer
constructed and served people. The migration of the Chinese brought in th
concept of clan association to Tekong Island. It was the support of fellov
townsmen that assisted Chinese to explore foreign lands without any fea
thus the construction of clan association was vital. Guangdong & Fujia
Association offered a place for information exchange between migrant
from the same hometown and assistance as well. On the other hand, th

---

[76]Lianhe Zaobao (Singapore), 9 September 2007.

munity center erected by People's Action Party also provided space for ɪders' entertainment, though it was different from the association.

As the saying goes, "Rome was not built in a day," and this was the of educational institutions on Tekong. Since the Chinese stressed on importance of education, there were six different primary schools in ∎ous phases so that ethnic education could be passed on from generation ∎eneration. With increase in the number of residents on the island, the ﹄ for medical institutions was gaining importance, and the government ɔrdingly established clinics to meet people's need. This chapter explores way of life in different villages and ethnic groups on Tekong Island. ﹍ discussion also involves religion, education, associations and medical ﹍itutes, which are important in understanding the life on Tekong Island. ﹍llage can be regarded as a mix of cultures. Cultural differences exist even ﹍in one ethnic group, while interaction among different ethnic groups may ﹍lt in the same culture. In Tekong Island villages, the movement, conflict, ﹍gration and development of the society were significantly correlated with relationship among ethnic groups. Chapter 3 investigates the distribution relationship among ethnic groups on Tekong Island.

CHAPTER 3

Composition and Relationship of Ethnic Groups

h an area of 24.4 km², Tekong Island is used as a training base and hosts
Basic Military Training Center. Before 1987, there were around 4,000 to
0 residents on the island. There are two versions about how this island's
1e came into being. Prior to the migration of Malays, the island was
:en, so it was called Pulau Tukung.[1] In the other version, Tekong Island
situated at the mouth of the Johor River, and therefore was named as
kong", which means "fortress".[2] These two names are not contradictory
he former signified the migrants' first impression of the island and the
er name was given by the migrants after they settled down. The presence
.n island's name denotes human inhabitation. The Chinese and Malays
ned a society of migrants on the island, which can be considered as an
ome of the Singapore's society.

As mentioned in the Chapter 2, the Malays moved to Tekong Island
! established their new homeland because of the civil war in 19th century
Malaya. After mid-19th century, the island required a huge workforce
the British government to commence the island's development. Due
insufficient human resources, the colonial government was forced to
:uit outside labor force. Some Chinese who lived in faraway areas were
:acted and left their hometowns, going southward. Some of the Chinese
ived in Singapore and some in Tekong Island to start their new lives.
ferent ethnic groups came to the island and lived together, resulting in
interaction between different groups and cultures. In addition to the
lays and Chinese, there were various Chinese ethnic groups, including
kka, Chaozhou, Fujian, Hainan and Guanfu. It was the diversity within
: Chinese community that stimulated the ethnic relationships and cultural
eractions.

This chapter explores the rapport between the Chinese and Malays on
kong Island, their cultural interactions and the inter-Chinese relationships,

---

e term "Tukung" means being barren according to the definition in dictionary *Kamus Dewan*
lished by Dewan Bahasa dan Pustaka. Iskandar, T. (1986) *Kamus Dewan*, p. 1291. Kuala
npur: Dewan Bahasa dan Pustaka.
andar, T (1986). *Kamus Dewan*, p. 1214. Kuala Lumpur: Dewan Bahasa dan Pustaka.

including how the Hakka, who constituted the largest Chinese ethnic grou
got along with the Chaozhouese. This chapter focuses on whether t
presence of varied ethnic groups resulted in integration or conflict duri
the development of the island.

3.1. Ethnic Structure on Tekong Island

Before the ethnic structure on Tekong Island is discussed, the concept
"ethnic group" is first introduced. As the term "ethnic group" originat
late in the English language, it had not been widely used until 1950s to 196(
The terms "race" and "nation"[3] were used more often to describe a simil
concept. The Taiwanese scholar Wang Fu Chang (王甫昌) elaborates that

> an ethnic group can be considered categories of human. People may wonder,
> among all human beings, who are related to them and what kind of relationship
> it is; "ethnicity" is one of the relationships. It can be imagined that, in a society
> or a nation, a group of people who share the same origin is categorized in the
> same ethnic group. Though "this ethnic group" and "that ethnic group" can
> thus be distinguished, the most interesting thing is that all ethnic groups are
> made of "people." In other words, the difference between ethnic groups comes
> from cultures. There is no ethnic group superior or better than another one; only
> differences exist between groups. It is expected that people show respect to the
> culture and features of different ethnic groups and even assist endangered ethnic
> groups in preserving their culture.[4]

We agree with Wang that ethnic groups are supposed to respect eac
other instead of being hostile. After the immigrants from China and Mala
Peninsula migrated to Tekong Island, would different cultures and religior
cause a positive or negative influence? Before this issue is discussed, the
ethnic structure and villages are first introduced.

The population on Tekong Island mainly comprised people of Chines
and Malay origin. Based on the census in 1957, there were 4,169 peopl
on the island, including 2,425 Chinese descents, 1,692 Malays, 44 Indiar
and Pakistanis and 8 people[5] of other ethnic groups. Except for th
decreased population,[6] the ethnic structure had not changed greatly accorc
ing to the research conducted in 1969 by the Department of Geograph
of Nanyang University: 2,337 Chinese descents, 1,679 Malays and onl

---

[3]Zhang, MG (张茂桂) (1999), Chapter 8: Race and Ethnicity. In *Sociology and Taiwan Societ*
Wang, ZH (王振寰) and Chu, HY (瞿海源) (eds.), pp. 239–279. Taipei: Chuliu Publisher.
[4]Wang, FC (2003). *Ethnic Imagination in Contemporary Taiwan*, p. 20. Taipei: Socio Publishin
[5]*Report on the Census of Population 1957* (1964). p. 109. Singapore: Government Printer.
[6]The number of residents on Tekong Island did not rise but declined after 12 years. It was probabl
because people tended to earn their livelihood in Singapore.

lians.[7] The census in 1957 was carried out to calculate the population in
apore rather than the population of separate areas. Therefore, the ethnic
cture of Chinese descent on Tekong Island was unknown only by the
us. On the other hand, the research conducted by Nanyang University
Tekong Island as the object of study and offered detailed popula-
statistics. The research showed that more than 50% of the Chinese
ents on the island are Hakka, up to 1,444, followed by 800 descents
haozhou immigrants, 48 from Hainan Island, 43 from Fujian and only
antonese.

Why was Hakka the biggest ethnic group within Chinese? Among the
nese in Singapore, people from Fujian accounted for around 45% but
Hakka constituted only 7%.[8] The reason was that people from Fujian
e powerful in the field of business, including banking, insurance and
ber processing and manufacturing.[9] As Fujian businessmen controlled
e resources compared to others, it was easier for their fellow townsmen
ind work in Singapore with help from friends and relatives. Accordingly,
ple from Fujian had the advantage of huge human resources, financial
ability and the power to make policies among Chinese as well.[10] Hence,
y were provided many opportunities in Singapore rather than Tekong
nd. Hakka constituted a minority in Singapore and had less power than
se from Fujian, so Tekong Island became a place for them to earn their
lihood.

Despite being a small island with only few thousands of residents, there
e various ethnic groups on the island, including Malay and Chinese and
erent subsects within Chinese; multiplicity of ethnic groups is one of the
ures of Tekong Island. The presence of different ethnic groups is always a
rce of ethnic tension and conflict and leads to social problems. Whether
difference among these ethnic groups on Tekong Island led to peace and
tual respect or conflict is investigated in the next sections.

---

i, ZB (1971). *Population and usage of land on Tekong Island*, p. 8. Unpublished honors thesis,
yang University, Dept. of Chinese Studies.
cording to the census in 1957, the number of Singaporeans was 1,090,596, and that of Fujian
e over 500,000 but Hakka were only around 78,000. *Report on the Census of Population 1957*
i4), p. 146. Singapore: Government Printer.
ng, CF (杨进发) (1999). *Tan Kah-Kee: The Making of an Overseas Chinese Legend.* [Translated
Lee, FC (李发沉)]. p. 10. US: Bafang Corp. World Scientific.
uring the time when Tan Kah Kee was the chairman of Fujian clan association, he was also
chairman of Ee Hoe Hean Club, the board chairman of the rubber association in Singapore
the board chairman of Nanyang Siang Pau. Yong, CF (杨进发) (1999). *Tan Kah-Kee: The
king of an Overseas Chinese Legend.* [Translated by Lee, FC (李发沉)] pp. 153–185. US: Bafang
p. World Scientific.

3.2. Relationship Between Chinese and Malays

3.2.1. *Population distribution of Chinese and Malays*

In the 19th century, Tekong Island was the ideal location, and undevelop
lands on the island attracted Malays and Chinese who, therefore, were t
primary ethnic groups on the island. In order to gain a better understandi
of these groups, it is necessary to understand how two ethnic groups wi
different cultures, languages, and religions got along for over a century
one island. There were 14 villages and 1 estate on Tekong Island and t
number of Chinese and Malays is shown in Table 1.

It is clear from Table 1 that Kampong Sungei Belang, Kampong Ay
Samak and Chia Tong Quah Estate comprised only the Chinese, who al
accounted the most, 330, in Kampong Seminei in which there were only
Malays. In Kampong Pahang, most residents were Malays while there we
only 34 Chinese. As for other groups, the number of Chinese and Mala
were almost the same in some villages or comprised 30% to 70% to in othe
There were up to 10 villages with both Chinese and Malay residents. Tl
Chinese and Malays interacted very often in economical, cultural and dai
activities. How and to what degree the interaction influenced the lives of tv
ethnic groups would be discussed in Sec. 3.2.2.

Table 1. Number of Chinese and Malay residents in each village on Tekong Island.

Village	Total number of the resident	Number of Chinese	Number of Malays
Kampong Selabin	789	574	215
Kampong Permatang	253	81	172
Kampong Pasir Merah	103	45	58
Kampong Unum	240	131	109
Kampong Sungei Belang	90	90	0
Kampong Ayer Samak	116	116	0
Kampong Pasir	119	68	51
Kampong Pengkalan Pakau	205	100	105
Kampong Sanyongkong Parit	281	210	71
Kampong Sanyongkong	205	141	64
Kampong Batu Koyok	232	171	61
Kampong Ladang	222	85	137
Kampong Seminei	337	330	7
Kampong Pahang	663	34	629
Chia Tong Quah Estate	161	161	0
Total	**4,016**	**2,337**	**1,679**

Source: Wu, ZB (1971). Population and usage of land on Tekong Island. Unpublished honors thesis, Nanyang University.[11]

---

[11]There were only three Indians on the island; one was in Kampong Pahang and other two wer
in Kampong Selabin. Indians are not listed in the table due to small number.

2. Interaction between Chinese and Malays

Malays established their villages on Tekong Island earlier than Chinese how did the Malays get along with the increasing number of Chinese on island? As the relationship among ethnic groups has been an important ≥ in a society, even in a country, this section focuses on these two ethnic ips on the island. The Chinese scholar Ma Rong maintains that:

A country is able to consolidate people's cohesion via internal racial integration if it can well handle the issue of ethnic relationship. Thus, the cost of social management is lower, the efficacy of social and economic organization is raised and the whole country is more prosperous... On the contrary, the vicious circle of contradiction among ethnic groups will widen the distance between people if ethnic relationship is not properly dealt with... The whole society will eventually break down if the contradiction becomes political conflict and movement of disintegration... All ethnic groups in this country will be "loser" under such circumstance.[12]

A leader of a country is supposed to consider a way to tackle the issue nultiplicity of ethnic groups and their development. The migration of nese and Malays made Tekong Island a multiethnic society, where these ethnic groups had lived together for over a century without any conflict, ch became one of characteristics of the island. Malays, who comprised second largest ethnic group on the island, had always served the post he village head, especially the second village head, Tengku Ahmad bin igku Sulong, who was assigned in 1949 by the colonial government as village head of Tekong Island and its outlying islets, such Pulau Tekong :il, Ubin Island, Serangoon Island, Ketam Island, Sejahat Island, Unum nd and Sanyongkong Island. On 6 June 1952, the colonial government i appointed by British Queen to develop Singapore.[13] As the government not pay much attention to a small island with only few thousands of idents, Tengku Ahmad bin Tengku Sulong was granted much power to e the island. Since Tengku Ahmad bin Tengku Sulong treated everyone ially despite his ethnicity, he was highly respected by all ethnic groups on island. According to the islanders' oral statements about the history, all idents highly praised Tengku Ahmad bin Tengku Sulong and recognized contribution to maintaining peace Tekong Island.[14]

la, R (马戎) (2006). New thoughts of understanding ethnic group: avoiding politicization on Minorities, In *Ethnicity and Society*, Wu, TT (吴天泰) (ed.), p. 80. Taipei: Wu-Nan Book Inc.
'engku Ahmad's 1949 Letter of Appointment. Singapore: Malay Heritage Center.
)ral History Interview with Loo Geuang Fiyau (2007). Singapore: Tekong Island Project; *Oral tory Interview with Huang Sheng Jie* (2007). Singapore: Tekong Island Project; *Oral History* :rview with Jaffar bin Kassim (2008). Singapore: Tekong Island Project.

Head of village of Tekong Island Tengku Ahmad bin Tengku Sulong (third from left, frc row) represented the inhabitants to give flag to MP of Changi Robin Sim (third from rig) front row).

The residents on Tekong Island realized the spirit of mutual aid. F instance, islanders helped each other fix fishing nets when strong wind prevented fishing; Chinese and Malays gifted each other poultry or hom made cake during Chinese New Year (or Muslim holidays) for celebration[1] whenever residents needed assistance like repairing house or roof, neighbo chipped in to help.[16] It was the affection of hundreds of years between the ethnic groups on the island, not the government's policy or outside forc that contributed the island's harmony.

The birthday of Tuan on lunar 5 December was a big event on Tekor Island and was a day of celebration for the Chinese. The Malays' influenc on the Chinese religion could be gleamed from some specific features, such a Tuan's image and way of address. Men were addressed as "Tuan" in Mala Furthermore, why did "Pokung" and "Da Pokung"[17] relate to Hakka?

In Taiwan's early history, the Hakka, who mainly relied on agricultur were closely connected to Pokung, the God of Earth, in their daily live

---

[15] *Oral History Interview with Loo Geuang Fiyau* (2007). Singapore: Tekong Island Project; *On History Interview with Huang Sheng Jie* (2007). Singapore: Tekong Island Project; *Oral Histo Interview with Lea Guan Chong* (2007). Singapore: Tekong Island Project.

[16] *Oral History Interview with HD Yusop bin Kasim* (1984). Singapore: Oral History Departmen

[17] The Hakka in Taiwan called the god of Earth as "Pokung". The Hakka in Singapore and Malaysi raised its status calling it "Da Pokung" ("Da" means "big" in Chinese) and respect it equally a the goddess of mercy. For example, Da Pokung was worshipped as main god in Fook Tet So Hakka Temple (望海大伯公) in Singapore and Supreme Old Lord (太上老君) is worshipped insid temple.

example, in the Hakka village in Pingtong, the elderly villagers burned
nse in Pokung temple every day, respectfully presenting three cups of
r and cleaning the temple.[18] When the Hakka migrated to southeastern
, they brought their beliefs to the new country (Pokung is called Da
ung in Southeast Asia). There have been many publications introducing
relationship between Da Pokung and Hakka, such as *History of Da
ung* by Han Huai Chun (韩槐准) in 1940, *Da Pokung, Erh Pokung
Pen Toukung* by Xu Yun Qiao (许云樵) in 1951, *History of Tokong
Tan Koh Kee* (陈育崧), *Studying Da Pokung* by Xu Yun Qiao in 1952,
oduction of Pokung* by Jao Tsung I (饶宗颐), *Origing of Da Pokung and
Taipo* by Xu Yun Qiao in 1956 and *Da Pokung on Penang Island and
chu Island* by Kuang Guo Xiang (邝国祥) in 1957. After that, several
lars researched this topic: *Who is Da Pokung* by Tien Guanci (天官赐)
963, *God of Three Names: Da Pokung, Na Tukung and God of Earth*
Yao Huang (黄尧) in 1981, and *Relationship between Da Pokung, Na
ung and God of Earth* by Zhang Shao Kuan (张少宽) in 1982. In the 21st
ury, there are three articles related to this field: *Chinese's God of Earth
Worship of Holy Relics in Southeastern Asia — Da Pokung in Malaysia*
Tan Chee Beng (陈志明), *A Study of Da Pokung and Worship of Earth
Chinese in Southeastern Asia — A Case of Thailand* by Gao Wei Nong
伟浓) and *Development of Da Pokung in Hakka Society in Southeastern
a* by Tan Chee Beng.

The above publications regarded Pokung either as a god defending
land or the ancestor of Chinese, and these two identities are closely
ted to the religion in Chinese society because Chinese worship both gods
their ancestors. Take the God of Earth for example, who had been
theosized and localized to be closer to people's life and became not so
sterious since Spring and Autumn Period and Warring States Period.
lier, ancestors who contributed to the society were worshipped as gods
later, virtuous people were also consecrated in a temple. Eventually
ple with morality were worshipped locally.[19] It can be seen that no
tter whether a government official or an ordinary person, anyone could
worshipped as a god of land as long as the person contributed to the
ld or people. Da Pokung in Hakka society evolved from the same style
religion. In Taiwan and southeastern Asia, the Hakka called the spirits
y worshipped as "Pokung" or "Da Pokung," by which people show their

ai, MK (蔡明坤) and Wang, SH (王淑慧) (2005). *The Pokung Temple in Hakka Village in Liutui
Neipu*. p. 1. Taipei: Council for Hakka Affairs, Executive Yuan & SMC Publishing Inc.
in, W (殷伟) (2003). *Gods in Chinese Religion*, p. 52. Kunming (昆明): Yunnan People
lishing.

respect in using such personalized address. The Taiwanese scholar Zhen Z
Ming maintains in his paper that "Pokung" is a form of address of the elde
or the ancestor in Hakka society. The title, when used to address gods, sho
the level of intimacy between the people and the spirits they worship.[20]
can be discovered that Hakka involved land worship along with worshippi
their ancestors, so Da Pokung is equipped with two identities: the God
Earth and the virtuous ancestor.

The chaos in late Qing Dynasty compelled the migration of people
parts of Hakka region to southeastern Asia and the belief in Pokung, the G
of Earth, also spread to their new settlements. In order to further identi
the relationship between the Hakka and Pokung, it is necessary to pro
into which Pokung temples in Singapore and Malaysia were built by Hakk
when they were established and what the purpose was.

There is an old temple located beside the most prosperous commerci
area in Singapore, Shenton Way, and this temple has existed in Singapo
for a long time. With the development in Singapore, Fook Tet S
Hakka Temple, (望海大伯公) constructed by the Hakka from Five Counti
of Jiaying (嘉应) [Mei County, Pingyuan, Xingning, Wuhua and Jiɛ
Ling (梅县、平远、兴宁、五华、蕉岭)] and Three Counties of Feng Yung
(丰永大) (Fongxun, Yongding and Dapu), was almost forgotten. Accordir
to archives, this temple was built by the Hakka from eight counties in 184
Prior to the construction of this temple, Da Pokung had been worshippe
by the Hakka since Stamford Raffles arrived in Singapore, based on th
statements of the elder Hakka. With increasing number of pilgrims, th
people decided to construct a temple for Da Pokung; this temple has laste
for 186 years and is the oldest Pokung temple in Singapore.

In Malaysia, the temple of Da Pokung is on Hai Chu Soo (珠海屿) i
Penang. The inscription of the stele states that Da Pokung was apotheos
of three Hakka ancestors, Zhang Li (张理), Qiu Zhao Jin (丘兆进) and Ma F
Chun (马福春), who migrated from Chaozhou to Batavia (Jakarta today) k
boat but were blown off to Penang by a hurricane. They stayed in Penan
and reclaimed the land; their tombstones were situated near the temple. Th
inscription on Chang's stone regarded him a "pioneer of exploring". Thi
temple, combined people's respect for their ancestors and the God of Eartl
was established by the Hakka from Yongding (永定), Dapu (大埔), Huizho
(惠州), Zeng Cheng (增城) and Jiaying (嘉应) in 1990 and was considered a
a local guardian god by the Hakka from the five counties. The Hakka jointl

---

[20]Zheng, ZM (郑志明) (2004). Development of Da Pokung in Hakka Society in Southeastern Asia
Huaqiao University Journal (华侨大学学报), **1**, 65.

the rights to manage the temple and regularly hold rituals. That the
stors are worshipped as the god of earth corresponds to the fact that
ka are involved in ancestral worship.

The relationship between Hakka and Pokung can be seen from the above
ription. The worship of Tuan by the residents on Tekong Island can be
rded as a combination of Keramat, a guardian god in non-Muslim areas,
Pokung. Legend has it that Tuan was a general of Aceh Kingdom in
 century and he was defeated by Portuguese army (see Sec. 2.2). It was
ored that the spirit of the general often wandered on Sejahat Island so
 islanders named a huge stone on the island Tuan Pokung. After leaving
ong Island, people from Chaozhou built Tuan Kong Beo Temple and
ded to shape a golden body for Tuan. The reason was that the huge
e on Sejahat Island was seen as a replacement for the spirit, who had
golden body. As the people were not able to return to Sejahat Island
worship, a golden body was needed for worship. The committee of the
ple decided on Tuan's image after lengthy discussion and accepting input
 the residents. Even now, on every lunar 15 December, Tuan's portrait
ws that he wears a crescent-shaped chapeau, traditional Chinese dressing
 Malaysian sarong with a beard and benign look on his face, seated
 his legs crossed. Besides the portrait, couplets were written in praise:
an illuminates for thousands of year, his merits and virtues radiating tens
housands of generations." This portrait was embroidered by a Chinese
ter in 1997, representing a holy image combined with the beliefs of both
Chinese and Malays.

Nevertheless, it is not clear why Hakka were not concerned with any
al for worshipping Tuan after leaving Tekong Island while Chaozhouese
red no effort in establishing clan associations to connect with fellow
nsmen. As Chaozhou Tuan Pokung Temple was constructed by people
n Chaozhou, the annual Pokung's birthday ceremony was also held by
 organization. According to the information provided by Ho Kim Fong,
 12 January 1985, representatives from Tian Kong Buddhist Temple,
angdong & Fujian Association and Chaozhou Corporation held a meeting
 the community center of Kampong Selabin. People participating in
 meeting comprised Dai Liou Niang (戴六娘), Wen Min Jun (温敏君),
en Rui Fa (陈瑞发), Wang Sou Qing, Lu Mou Ming (卢茂明), Tang Wan
g (汤挽平) and Ho Kim Fong. Most representatives from Tian Kong
ddhist Temple also represented Guangdong & Fujian Association such
 Tang and Ho; Wang and Lu took part in the meeting on behalf of
aozhou Corporation as well. Only Huang Hsiti represented Chaozhou
rporation alone. A member of the parliament of the Changi Constituency,

Teo Chong Tee (张宗治), was also invited to the meeting. At that tin
Tang suggested Tuan not be worshipped separately in Guangdong & Fuji
Association and Chaozhou Corporation after it was carried to Singapore b
Chaozhou Corporation did not agree with it. The director of Guangdo
& Fujian Association cast divining blocks, inquiring if Tuan was willi
to follow its believers to Singapore and the response was negative. Aft
islanders left Tekong Island in 1987, the director of Guandong & Fuji
Association, together with musicians, took a boat to Sejahat Island eve
lunar 15 December to worship and play music for three hours in order
offer their thanks to Tuan. The ritual had lasted until the 11 Septemb
attacks in 2001, after which Sejahat Island was taken over by the Minist
of National Defense and any activities on the island were banned.[21]

Celebrations of the birth of "Tuan" held by residents of Tekong Island.

Before leaving Tekong Island, Chinese on the island plunged in financi
and human resources, holding Tuan's birthday ceremony on every luna
15 December. On this day, the Chaozhou Company would be hired t
perform in Kampong Selabin. Representatives of Guangdong & Fujia
Association and Chaozhou Corporation, together with six musicians in th
theatrical company (three for gong and three for suona horn), took a boa
to Sejahat Island, welcoming Tuan to see the performance on Tekong Islanc
Tuan was sent back few days after the birthday celebrations.[22] As Tuan'

---

[21]Information provided by Ho Kim Fong.
[22]Residents on Tekong Island worshipped Tuan Pokung only in Guangdong & Fujian Associatior
Chaozhou Corporation or their own home rather than going to Sejahat Island in case disturb
ing Tuan.

ıday was extremely important to the Chinese, they paid much attention
his day and celebrated it with great pomp and fervor. The Malays also
their cakes and food, taking part in the celebrations. Tuan's birthday
only created a cordial atmosphere on the island but also stimulated
:action between ethnic groups. However, some Malays still believed the
ization was actually tantamount to devil worship.[23]
Religion and ethnicity are two sensitive issues in many countries and may
g about disorder if they are not handled well. Sometimes, international
lict, even wars, occurs due to religion and ethnic problems and cause
ı to the country and its people, such as Israel and other Muslim countries
liddle East. The sensitivity and complexity of these two issues always
e the ruler to ponder over a solution. On Tekong Island, regardless of the
tence of various ethnic groups on the same island, there has not been any
flict or war but only peace and mutual respect for over a century. It could
.een that Chinese temples and Malay mosques peacefully co-existed, and
ses of Muslim doctrine could also be found in Kampong Sanyongkong,
ıre the Hakka accounted for the majority. Furthermore, these ethnic
ıps also communicated in different languages. Most of the Chinese on
island were able to speak Malay language and some Malays could speak
ska,[24] which all reflected harmony on the island. After Singapore was
ıpied by Japan, the Malays on Tekong Island endeavored to protect the
nese from the Japanese.[25] Tekong Island was also free from the ethnic
ıding conflict in Singapore in 1964, which could be attributed to the
ıdship between Chinese and Malays for over a century.

The way Chinese perceived education also influenced the Malays. In the
 Qing Dynasty, domestic chaos and foreign invasion compelled people in
 coastal areas to leave their hometowns and migrate to Southeast Asia,
luding Tekong Island. Most migrants were disadvantaged in the society
l the hardships and difficulties they were facing in a strange environment
·e beyond measure. They hence recognized that education was the only
h for their children to get rid of poverty. Once they were aware of the
portance of education, they tried to construct schools with the money they
·ed. On Tekong Island, the Chinese endeavored to establish schools with
·ir economic resources for the purpose of cultivating their posterity. Some
ılays admired the way Chinese constructed schools, sending their children

ıral History Interview with HD Yusop bin Kasim (1984). Singapore: Oral History Department.
ıral History Interview with Jaffar bin Kassim (2008). Singapore: Tekong Island Project; Oral
tory Interview with Antung Lee (2007). Singapore: Tekong Island Project.
ıral History Interview with Chin Sit Har (1987). Singapore: Oral History Department.

to Chinese school, including H. J. Selong bin Embok Kating, YaYah a
Jaffar bin Kassim.[26]

Among the children educated in Chinese schools, Jaffar bin Kass
was influenced greatly by Chinese education and even became a brid
of communication between Chinese and Malays. Born on 13 August 19
in Kampong Pasir, Jaffar's father was a resident on Tekong Island a
his mother was a Bugi from Indonesia. As Jaffar's father recognized t
importance of Chinese, he transferred Jaffar from the Malay school to
Wah School. Fond of Chinese after graduation from primary school, Jaff
chose to study further in Whampoa High School (黄埔中学) in Singapo
because there was no high school on Tekong Island. After graduation,
was admitted to the Chinese Department of Nanyang University as the fir
Malay student. Jaffar had worked in Singapore Muslim council for 25 yea
after graduation from university.[27]

Influenced by both Malay and Chinese cultures, Jaffar had a de
understanding of the Chinese and Malay society. As a former resident o
Tekong Island, he utilized his talents to enhance the interaction between tv
ethnic groups and was aggressively involved in many activities, promotii
Chinese and Malay interaction. For instance, when Chinese visited Mal
Heritage Center, Jaffar explained Malay associations, religion, Hari Ra
Puasa, Hari Raya Haji, Malay customs and taboos of Muslims to Chine
in English.[28] Furthermore, Jaffar worked hard in enhancing the interactic
of cultures and popularizing Chinese culture. He established Yelin Languag
Center, providing students and Chinese adults, Malay and Arabic course
and helped mosques teaching Chinese. Al-Muttaqin was the first mosqu
providing a Chinese course with Jaffar's assistance. Jaffar stated, "I arrange
the course. The preliminary course taught student syllables of Chines
words and basic conversation like greetings, self-introduction, date, tim
conversation in phone and in shopping. I also talk about Chinese history an
culture in the first class. There are 90 students in Chinese course, from 1
to 60. They come from different fields in the society, including students fro
institutes of engineering, teachers, retired people, businessmen, housewive
youth, etc."[29] According to a report, the Chinese course had attracted a lc
of people and there were still some registrants who were not able to atten
the class due to space constraints.

---

[26] *Oral History Interview with Lea Guan Cheng* (2007). Singapore: Tekong Island Project; *Or
History Interview with Huang Wen De* (黄文德) (2007). Singapore: Tekong Island Project.
[27] *Oral History Interview with Jaffar bin Kassim* (2008). Singapore: Tekong Island Project.
[28] *Clan Association Journal*, **22** (2006).
[29] *Lianhe Zaobao* (Singapore), 28 March 2005.

The interaction and harmony between ethnic groups on Tekong Island
not disappear as residents left the island but was carried to Singapore by
ar and other residents. The government did not intentionally promote any
to improve the relationship between ethnic groups nor did any politician
to evoke the sensitive issue of ethnicity. There was not any conflict but
e on the island so that a harmonious society could be formed for various
ic groups on Tekong Island.

Though the respect between Chinese and Malays was praiseworthy, there
inevitably some friction between these two groups. During the period
n Japan occupied Tekong Island, a person of Chaozhou origin asked one
is relatives, a government agent, to take revenge on behalf of him as he
bullied by a Malay. The Malay was hence captured and beaten cruelly on
street. The incident triggered Malays' dissatisfaction and a crowd gath-
in Kampong Selabin asking for justice. Eventually people involved were
sted by Japanese soldiers to be examined and this incident was quelled.[30]
s small conflict did not affect the relationship between Chinese and Malays.
he following section, the relationship within Chinese would be explored to
erstand how the different Chinese groups got along with each other.

. Ethnic Relationship within Chinese

nese comprised the biggest group on Tekong Island, consisting of Hakka,
ozhouese, Fujian, Guangdong, and Hainan. The ethnic structure was
ilar to that in Singapore; the only difference was that the migrants
n Fujian accounted for the majority in Singapore while Hakka was
dominant group in Tekong Island. Among all villages on the island,
re were ten villages and one estate in which the number of Hakka was
re than any other groups, while the Chaozhouese were predominant only
three villages. Hakka and Chaozhouese alone accounted for more than
% of Chinese population on Tekong Island. As the Chinese from Fujian,
angdong and Hainan were quite few on the island (see Table 2), the focus
n the relationship between Hakka and Chaozhouese, and the other three
ups are ignored. If the occupation and the location of residence were
mined, the number of Hakka engaged in business was fewer, and most
them lived inland, planting rubber and vegetables and breeding poultry
a living. As for Chaozhouese, they lived along the coast and made their
ng by selling grocery and local products or fishing.[31]

---

ral History Interview with Heng Siew Hiok (王守旭) (1984). Singapore: Oral History Department.
ral History Department (1990). *Recollections: People and Places*, p. 61. Singapore: Oral History
artment.

Table 2.   Number of Chinese of different groups in each village on Tekong Island.

Village/Migrants	Hakka	Chaozhouese	Fujianese	Cantonese	Hainan
Kampong Selabin	239	308	4	2	21
Kampong Permatang	73	8	0	0	0
Kampong Pasir Merah	23	0	22	0	0
Kampong Unum	126	5	0	0	0
Kampong Sungei Belang	39	51	0	0	0
Kampong Ayer Samak	81	35	0	0	0
Kampong Pasir	48	20	0	0	0
Kampong Pengkalan Pakau	100	0	0	0	0
Kampong Sanyongkong Parit	188	22	0	0	0
Kampong Sanyongkong	113	28	0	0	0
Kampong Batu Koyok	103	68	0	0	0
Kampong Ladang	0	58	0	0	27
Kampong Seminei	118	195	17	0	0
Kampong Pahang	34	0	0	0	0
Chia Tong Quah Estate	159	2	0	0	0
Total	**1444**	**800**	**43**	**2**	**48**

Source: Wu, ZB (1971). Population and usage of land on Tekong Island, Unpublished honors thesis, Nanyang University.

Since the different Chinese groups shared the same ancestors and cultur is it necessary to further investigate the relationship within this ethn group? The difference within Chinese may be neglected if the whole Chines society was generalized. The statement of common ancestors and culture just a general record in Chinese history but there are still blurred areas fc different explanation of ethnicity. In the society of Singapore and Malaysia there are only Chinese and non-Chinese. Among the Chinese, they ar distinguished by the place of origin, such as Hakka, people from Chaozhou Fujian, or Hainan. Hence, the Chinese society is roughly divided into Han an other groups. Although Chinese share many common features in differen ways, there are differences. For example, there are ethnic problems in Taiwa even though nearly 98% people in Taiwan are Han. If the issue is impute to politicians' manipulation, their ability is overestimated and people autonomy and rationality are underestimated.[32] The way in which four mai

---

[32]Wang, FC. *Ethnic Imagination in Contemporary Taiwan*, p. vii. Taipei: Socio Publishing.

ic groups in Taiwan (South Fujianese, Hakka, Mainlanders, and the
igine) are categorized[33] depends on the time their ancestors appeared
aiwan. The Taiwanese scholar Wang Fu Chang proposes that:

The so-called four main groups in Taiwan, including the aborigine, Hakka, South
Fujianese (Fulaoren) and Mainlander, are actually categorized by three contrary
ways. People are divided into the aborigine and Han; Han is divided into Islander
and Mainlander; Islander is again divided into South Fujianese and Hakka.[34]

In terms of identity, the Hakka and migrants considered themselves
nese when facing the Malays. The terms "Hakka" and "Chaozhou"
mentioned only when it comes to the difference within Chinese, their
juages, and historical experience. As the relationship between ethnic
ips is emphasized, the connection between Hakka and Chaozhouese can
be observed by probing into their interactions.

The society on Tekong Island comprised various villages with only few
isands of residents. Each household was familiar with others, and people
along with each other very well. Whenever there was a joyous occasion
a funeral, neighbors would go to help whoever needed. According to a
ner islander, every household would receive a red candle if a person
sed away. The red candle was lit in front of the house at the night of
funeral to lighten a path for the deceased to another world.[35] Residents
sted each other not only in weddings or funerals but also in rituals or
holidays. The bond between people on the island relied on their affection
friendship, which were rarely seen in cities. Regardless of the affections,
re was inevitably conflict among people.

The first Chinese association on Tekong Island, Guangdong & Fujian
ociation, was established in late 19th century by businessmen and
downers. The progress of businessmen was closely related to the policy of
onial government in Malaya, which actively encouraged commercial activ-
s and offered many opportunities to promote business.[36] Gradually, the
sinessmen formed their own circle and some of them became leaders in the

---

owadays there are five main groups in Taiwan: the original four main groups plus "new
rant," which refers to foreign brides from Indonesia, Vietnam and Mainland China.
'ang, FC. *Ethnic Imagination in Contemporary Taiwan*, p. 56. Taipei: Socio Publishing.
ral History Interview with Lea Guan Chong (2007). Singapore: Tekong Island Project;
rmation provided by Ho, KF.
tamford Raffles focused on the development of business and gave preferential treatment to busi-
smen. He protected businessmen's benefits and stated that they were the backbone of Singapore.
, XS (林孝胜) (1995). *Early Period of Chinese Society in Singapore*. In *Chinese Association*
Businessman, Lin, XS (ed.) p. 8. Singapore: Singapore Society of Asian Studies.

Chinese society.[37] The reason the colonial government encouraged busin∎ was for developing the economy. Since the Chinese businessmen had influer∎ to some extent in the society, they would further try to exercise their lead∎ ship in the society to advance the economic development. Such situations h∎ destroyed the Chinese tradition in which the society was led by scholars∎ Since the clan association and guild were guided by Chinese businessme∎ they were supposed to be responsible for promoting education. In this wa∎ they could be recognized by other people and maintain their influence a∎ reputation, fulfilling the duty to be a leader in the society. As the cl∎ association played significant role in Chinese education in Malaya, Chine∎ businessman, clan association, and Chinese education were closely corr∎ lated.[39] The development of Chinese schools had been funded by Chine∎ businessmen, the association and people who were concerned because∎ was not supported by the colonial government. For example, the Fuji∎ businessmen Tan Kah Kee and Tan Lark Sye (陈六使)[40] led Fujian Cl∎

---

[37]Yen, QW (颜清湟) (1992). *History of Overseas Chinese*, p. 150–151. Singapore: Singapore Soci∎ of Asian Studies.

[38]There were four classes of people in ancient China: scholars, farmers, artisans and traders. Amo∎ the four classes, the scholar was the most important one. Most people expected their child enteri∎ the state's bureaucracy by imperial examination as a family honor. Such thinking was still root∎ in people's mind even though it was becoming more and more difficult in Ming and Qing Dynast∎ due to rising population. Traders had great influence only in Spring and Autumn Period becau∎ most emperors emphasized agriculture and restrained trade in ancient China. Such situation h∎ not changed until 16th century. In Ming Dynasty, those who were not able to pass the imper∎ examination chose to be engaged in business. However, the status of traders was still much low∎ than scholars. See Yu, YS (余英时) (1987). *Ethics of Chinese Religion in Recent Period and t∎ Spirit of Trader*, pp. 117–121. Taipei: Linkingbooks.

[39]Chen, JT (1970). *Relationship between Chinese Businessman, Clan Association and Educatio∎ A Case Study of Nanyang University's Construction by Fujian Clan Association*, p. 3. Unpu∎ lished honors thesis, Nanyang University.

[40]Tan Lark Sye was born on 7 June 1897 in Jimei of Tong An County. His father, Tan Ying L∎ (陈缨麟), and mother, Lin, had seven children in his family and they were Ke Yi (科椅), Ke Q∎ (科寝), Wen Que (文确), Wen Ke (文科), Wen Zhi (文知), Lark Sye (六使) and Wen Zhang (文章∎ The Tans earned their living by agriculture. Due to poverty, Tan Lark Sye's brothers did not stu∎ at school and his third elder brother also quit school after their parents passed away. Thanks t∎ Tan Kah Kee, who founded a primary school in Jimei Township in 1913, Tan Lark Sye and h∎ younger brother were able to obtain free education. At that time, China was in turmoil and th∎ life was tough. Tan Wen Que could not go fishing due to weak physical condition. Ke Qin decide∎ to send Wen que to Singapore to make a living and his brothers went south sequentially excep∎ Ke Yi and Ke Qin. The Tans did not have any friends or relatives but could depend on only fello∎ townsmen. Tan Wen Que thus worked in Qian Yi Corporation as a clerk with help from cla∎ association, and Tan Lark Sye was also hired in Tan Kah Kee's company. During the seven yea∎ in Tan Kah Kee's company, Tan Lark Sye acquired much experience in work and managemen∎ which were important foundations for his business. Tan Lark Sye and his brothers founded Lie∎ he Rubber Corp. in 1923 and the company developed quite smoothly. Later they founded Yi b∎ Rubber Corp. in 1924 and gained great profit due to rising price of rubber in early 1950s. Tan Lar∎ Sye as well as other Chinese businessmen started their business from nothing but became a tycoo∎ by the spirit of overcoming hardships. Tan Lark Sye was hence aggressively engaged in educatio∎

ciation which constructed five schools, including Taonan School (道南), ong School (爱同), Chong Fu School (崇福), Nan Qiao School (南侨), and g Wah School (光华). Other examples included Qifa School (启发学校) ded by Liu, Chun Rong (刘春荣) from Char Yong (Dabu) Association 906.[41] Ying Fo Fui Kun (应和会馆) led by Thong Siong Lim (汤湘霖) established a school in 1904.[42] The Guangdong & Fujian Association, other associations in Singapore, was guided by businessmen and was onsible for taking care of fellow townsmen and developing education.

At an early phase, Guangdong & Fujian Association was jointly managed Iakka and Chaozhouese because these two groups had the advantage of ority. In the 1930s, Chaozhouese were not pleased that the association controlled by the Hakka so they started Chaozhou Corporation to keep ing their fellow townsmen.[43] As Tuan was worshipped in Chinese society Tekong Island, the annual ritual was originally held by Guangdong & an Association. Later Chaozhou Corporation and Guangdong & Fujian ociation, respectively, held rituals on the street in Kampong Selabin and d a theatrical company to show their gratitude to the god.[44] Both the ciations hired theatrical Chaozhou companies but "Han Opera" was available since there was no full-time opera company in Singapore so it replaced by "Chaozhou Opera," which was cheaper. Two rituals held ectively by Chaozhou Corporation and Guandong & Fujian Association ned to be in competition as the Hakka and Chaozhouese did not get ig that well according to Chin Sit Har, an old resident of Tekong Island.[45] other resident Ng Kia Cheu said, "two sides held their own opera. When ime here in the first year, the opera lasted until dawn. Two sides were peting."[46] It could be seen that two associations both tried to outshine h other. At that time, with a view of surpassing the other side, both ras even raised their volume and kids also tried to interrupt the other

---

charity and took the post as one of the members of the board of the five schools, chairman ujian Clan Association, director of Singapore Chinese Chamber of Commerce, chairman and gapore Rubber Association, chairman of Nanyang Post and etc.

har yong Association (ed.) (1958). *Singapore Memorial Journal for 100 Years of Char yong ociation*, p. 10. Singapore: Char Yong Association.

hen, JT, *Relationship between Chinese Businessman, Clan Association and Education: A Case dy of Nanyang University's Construction by Fujian Clan Association*, p. 18. Unpublished honor sis, Nanyang University.

ral History Interview with Heng Siew Leng (2007). Singapore: Tekong Island Project; *Oral tory Interview with Wang Sou Qing* (2007). Singapore: Tekong Island Project.

uangdong & Fujian Association built the stage on the street in Kampong Selabin while iozhou Corporation had the stage on the other side of the street (near the coast).

ral History Interview with Chin Sit Har (1987). Singapore: Oral History Department.

ral History Interview with Ng Kia Cheu (1982). Singapore: Oral History Department.

side by play tricks on the actors with fingers or tree branches.[47] Althou
the Hakka and Chaozhouese cooperated most of the time, there were s
some conflicts.

The Tuan Temple and spirit tablet of Tuan Temple (Small Icon) of Chaozhou Corporatio

    After World War II, although the Hakka and Chaozhouese joint
held Tuan's birthday ceremony, these two groups argued over the place
the incense burner. The Hakka believed that the Heavenly Lord's burne
which Hakka considered the most important, should be placed in the mo:
important place while Chaozhouese insisted that Tuan's burner be place
right in the middle because the purpose of the ceremony was the celebratio
of Tuan's birthday. In the end, the conflict was mediated by the village hea
Tengku Ahmad bin Tengku Sulong and both sides agreed to have Tuan
burner set in the middle.[48]
    The conflict between these two groups revealed the difference on religio
The Han people respect nature and the earth the most as they are closel
related to the crops in an agricultural society. Han people believe mothe
earth is grand, blessed, and sacred and it can be replaced by nothing

---

[47]Information provided by Ho, KF.
[48]*Oral History Interview with Heng Siew Leng* (2007). Singapore: Tekong Island Project; *Or*
History Interview with Wang Shou Qing (2007). Singapore: Tekong Island Project.

ordingly, Hakka face outside when worshipping the nature.[49] That was
the Hakka insisted that Heavenly God's incense burner be arranged
t in the middle on Tuan's birthday ritual in order to show the highest
us of the nature. By contrast, Chaozhouese personalized the heaven
respected it from human's perspective. Thus, on Tuan's birthday, they
ved Tuan was the most important figure so his incense burner should be
e in the middle instead of the Heavenly God's burner. There was nothing
t or wrong with the thinking of Hakka or Chaozhouese. Their conflict
inated from the difference in their concept of religion.

idents of Tekong Island took a boat to Sejahat Island to welcome the Tuan to Tekong
nd.

After the community center was constructed in 1963, the Hakka and
aozhouese also had disputes on the internal affairs. Prior to a party held
nhance the relationship among villagers, the representatives of both sides
e considering sponsoring this activity. Finally, the party was funded by
side of Chaozhou, and the Hakka did not put up any capital. On the day
he party, that the side of Chaozhou hung up a red banner "Sponsored by
aozhou Corporation" displeased the Hakka leader, who asked to rewrite
banner as "Sponsored by Chaozhou and Hakka." Some people from
side of Chaozou thought that Hakka just wanted publicity without
ering any financial support.[50] Although the two sides insisted on what

---

eng, XC (曾喜城) (1999). *Study on Hakka Culture in Taiwan*, p. 130. Taipei: National Taiwan
rary.
ral History Interview with Heng Siew Hiok* (1984). Singapore: Oral History Department.

they requested, peace was above everything to these two groups. In the er
the representative of Chaozhou side gave in to the Hakka's request.
The above incidents were just trivial conflicts because the Hakka a
Chaozhouese had always maintained a good relationship and assisted ea
other in times of need. Soon after World War II, the economic situation
Malaya and Singapore was still weak as the rubber industry, which peor
in two territories relied on for living, was seriously affected and its pri
thus greatly fell. From 1948 to 1949, rubber was worth only 30 cents p
pound.[51] Those Hakka who made the living by planting rubber were hen
influenced while Chaozhouese, who lived by fishing, were forced to move o
due to the impact. Due to economic difficulties, the Hakka was not capat
of hiring a theatrical company on Tuan's birthday so the Chaozhour
were responsible for the expenses of the opera. Former resident Ng K
Cheu recalled the economic situation of Tekong Island after World W
II, "Even though the economic situation was bad, Chaozhou could still ;
fishing. As for the Hakka, they all depended on farming, it was tough!"
The economic situation had not improved until the 1950s. In June 1950, t!
Korean War broke out, and the price of rubber climbed drastically becau
of the increase of demand on rubber.[53] With the rising price of rubbe
Hakka's income increased accordingly and hence they were able to affor
Tuan's birthday ceremony with Chaozhouese. Since then, both Hakka ar
Chaozhou hired opera companies, the opera lasted for two to five days. Ever
year a committee was organized to be in charge of related affairs of the oper
Since the Chaozhou Corporation had been responsible for Tuan's birthdz
ceremony for years after World War II, it would be Chaozhou Corporatior
which managed the opera, to show Hakka's respect to Chaozhouese and tl
mutual understanding of these two groups.

Hakka and Chaozhou, two groups that had migrated from the sout
of China to Tekong Island, had disagreements in the beginning. With tk
passage of time, the disagreement was gradually dissolved as they knew eac
other more and intermarriage also brought two groups together.[54] Becaur
the Hakka outnumbered the Chaozhouese, as well as due to the frequer
interaction in neighborhood and trade, most Chaozhouese on the island coul
speak Hakka and many Hakka people learned to speak Chaozhouese. Th

---

[51] After Korea War broke out in June 1950, the price of rubber started to rise. The price was up t
two dollars one pound in 1951. See Guo Ping (国平) (1962). *Rubber Industry in Malaya*, pp. 28–2!
34–35. Singapore: World Book Co., Ltd.
[52] *Oral History Interview with Ng Kia Chew* (1982). Singapore: Oral History Department.
[53] Wilson, J (1958). *The Singapore Rubber Market*, pp. 34–37. Singapore: Eastern Universitie
Press.
[54] *Oral History Interview with Heng Siew Hiok* (1984). Singapore: Oral History Department.

...ers between the two groups blurred and they integrated by marriage,
...ing from each other, and common life experiences, becoming a whole-
...e society on Tekong Island.

Conclusion

...society on Singapore was multiethnic while that on Tekong Island, with
...r population and the same ethnic structure, was like an epitome of
...apore. Multiplicity of races denotes multiplicity of language, culture,
...religion. The Chinese scholar Xu Gui Lan (徐桂兰) believes that
...her there are ethnic conflict, ethnic contradiction and even ethnic war
...ard vicious development or groups contact, interact and recognize with
...a other toward benign development in a nation with multiple ethnic
...ps."[55] It was inappropriate to dichotomize ethnic development as it was
...rlocked with cultural background, historical experiences of the ethnic
...ps and its living environment and the situation. Ethnic disagreement
...ontradiction does not absolutely lead to conflicts and interaction does
...ensure integration either. Take Malaya for example. Since the 1950s, the
...nese's goal of education had differed from that of Malays as the latter
...d to focus on giving more importance to Malay language in education
...le Chinese strived for an equal position of Chinese education. It was
...ious these two groups did not see eye to eye on this issue because the
...nese hindered Malays from realizing their target of Malay as the main
...guage in national education system. There were two reasons that no
...flict occurred before Malaya's independence. First, at that time, most
...ional affairs were controlled by the British government so the Malays did
...have the power to reform education or politics by their wish. Second,
...Malays tried to establish a peaceful atmosphere among all ethnic groups
...rder to be independent from the British. Therefore, Malays gave in to
...nese and Indians on many issues, including education so that other groups
...ld be willing to cooperate with the Malays. After the independence,
...nese and Malays still disagreed on politics, education and economy,
...their dispute finally resulted in bleeding conflicts, which was dissolved
...negotiation among leaders from every ethnic group. From Malaya's
...erience, it can be seen that there had been contradiction, conflict, and
...eraction in a multiethnic nation. However, the country has not been led
...integration yet.

...u, GL (徐桂兰) (2006). From Interaction to Integration — A Study on People in Hochou; In
nicity and Society, Wu, TT (ed.) p. 295. Taipei: Wu-Nan Book Inc.

As Tekong Island also had a multiethnic society, the ethnic structu was similar because Chinese and Malays on the island were accustom to each other. For example, some Chaozhouese once caused tension due personal resentment toward a Malay and gave rise to a conflict between t groups. In the early period, when Chinese migrated to the island, Hakka a Chaozhouese tended to have arguments because of trivial misunderstandin At that time, the chairman of Guangdong & Fujian Association, Chen Bi Kui (陈炳奎), often mediated the resolution of the argument. It is impossil for multiple ethnic groups living on the same island to not have any disput As different groups started to be accustomed to each other, they would lea how to understand and respect the other side so that the society could harmonious. However, it did not mean that all groups would be integrat because there were difference in religion, language, and culture. The be way of development was to cultivate admiration and respect for each oth like the Chinese and Malays on Tekong Island, who helped anyone in ne regardless of ethnicity. Even within the Chinese, people cooperated to bui their own homeland. Chin Sit Har composed a Hakka song to praise t spirit on Tekong Island: "From Selabin up to Sanyongkong, the road on t hill was rough. Residents paved the way together. On third and eighth lunar month, the rising tide washed away the bridge. Everybody offered the money and strength to fix the bridge."[56] Good relationships among grou brought harmony and peace to the society on Tekong Island. As a part Singapore, Tekong Island could not be excluded from the fate of Singapor In Chapter 4, which describes the period during the break out of Worl War II to Singapore's independence, the focus is on the influence on Tekor Island and how the islanders responded such radical changes in a period less than 50 years.

---

[56] Oral History Department (1990). *Recollections: People and Places*, p. 64. Singapore: Oral Histor Department.

CHAPTER 4

The Impact of World War II

; chapter explores the influence of the shift in Singapore's politics, society
economy on Tekong Island from the late 1930s to the mid-1960s. During
period, Singapore witnessed anti-Japanese movements, and Japan
ted the Pacific War and defeated the colonial army, thereby occupying
;apore. After the cessation of war, the colonial government returned to
;apore, which experienced a transition from semi–self-government to self-
ernment, while at the same time, the left wing rose to prominence. Later
;apore joined the Federation of Malaysia but became independent soon
rward. Furthermore, significant events such as the interaction between
ple's Action Party and the left wing also took place during this period.
: following sections examine the impact of Singapore's political events on
ong Island and the islanders' response to these events.

. Influence of World War II on Tekong Island

: Marco Polo Bridge Incident took place in northern China on the
ht of 7 July 1937. On 28 and 30 July, the Japanese army successively
upied Beijing and Tianjin. The Chinese leader Chiang Kai-shek issued
statement, "To all soldiers... since peace is hopeless, we can only
it to the end" and announced the beginning of the anti-Japanese war.
is news spread to the Chinese diaspora in Southeast Asia, including
ar, Kuala Lumpur, Ipoh, Penang and Alor Setar. Overseas Chinese
nediately arranged an organization to raise funds for the war.[1] On 15
gust, 700 representatives from 118 organizations in Singapore were slated
attend the meeting held by the Overseas Chinese. Later, 31 representatives
m different fields established the "Sin-Hua Fund Raising Organization
华筹帐会)." The first meeting of the organization was held at the Ee Hoe
an Club on 17 August, and Tan Kah Kee was selected as the chairman.[2]
n remained as the organizations' chairman until the eve of World War II.

---

ng, CF (1999). *Tan Kah-Kee: The Making of an Overseas Chinese Legend.* p. 226. Translated
Lee, FC. USA: Bafang Corp.
ng, CF (1999). *Tan Kah-Kee: The Making of an Overseas Chinese Legend.* p. 228. Translated
Lee, FC. USA: Bafang Corp.

The Chinese in Singapore plunged human and material resources in the war, which also influenced the residents of Tekong Island. To correspo with Tan Kah Kee, the Hakka and Chaozhouese on Tekong Island establish a branch of Sin-Hua Fund Raising Organization in September 1937, and t first chairman was Chen Rui Lin (陈瑞麟), who was also the chairman Guangdong & Fujian Association.[3] Senior leaders such as Huang Yi Hu (黄奕欢) and Hou Xi Fan (侯西反) arrived on the island, congratulati the establishment of the branch and praising the islanders' resolve fight against the Japanese army. Huang also called on the residents the island to provide financial assistance for the war.[4] At the prelimina phase of the fund-raising organization, the branch also published a month magazine[5] and formed a singing group to raise funds. The singing group Tekong Island sang songs against the atrocities of the Japanese in Hak and performed in major villages such as Kampong Selabin and Kampoi Sanyongkong. The anti-Japanese war awakened the society on Tekong Islai regardless of its population of a few thousands. Although the islanders we not able to raise a great deal of money, their determination to fight again Japan matched with that in Singapore.

Both the anti-Japanese war and the Pacific War were fought simult neously. The empire of Japan attempted to seize more resources and ci essential supplies to China. On 8 December 1941, Singapore was bombarde by Japan and couldn't retaliate as it lacked well-trained soldiers. The coloni government's morale collapsed while two principal vessels, HMS Repuls and HMS Prince of Wales, were destroyed by the Imperial Japanese Nav The Japanese army, led by the General Tomoyuki Yamashita, landed c the shores of Kota Bahru and proceeded to rapidly conquer the Mala Peninsula within two weeks.[6] The Singapore army resisted for one weel but Lieutenant-General A. E. Percival surrendered to the Japanese on I February 1942 as the Japanese threatened to cut water supply. As soon the Japanese army entered Singapore, it was renamed as Syonan Islanc which translated to "light of south." Furthermore, the Japanese soldie also started to persecute the Chinese for revenge. On 18 February 194 Sook Ching (肃清) was initiated to identify anti-Japanese elements. One c

---

[3] Oral History Interview with Chin Sit Har (1987). Singapore: Oral History Department.
[4] Oral History Interview with Ng Kia Cheu (1982). Singapore: Oral History Department.
[5] The monthly magazine reported news in simple language about the war and fund-raising activiti in Singapore. See Oral History Interview with Chin Sit Har (1987). Singapore: Oral Histor Department.
[6] Lee, YM (李玉梅) (1998). The Independence of Singapore. p. 28. Singapore: National Heritag Board.

most influential political figures, Lee Kuan Yew (李光耀), recalled the
nese violence as follows:

On 18 February, the Japanese put up notices and sent soldiers with loudspeakers
around the town to inform the Chinese that all men between the ages of 18 and 50
were to present themselves at five collection areas for inspection. The much-feared
Kempeitai went from house to house to drive Chinese who had not done so at
bayonet point to these concentration centers, into which women, children and old
men were also herded.... In theory, the Imperial Army could justify this action
as an operation to restore law and order and to suppress anti-Japanese resistance.
But it was sheer vengeance, exacted not in the heat of battle but when Singapore
had already surrendered. Even after this *Sook Ching*, there were mopping-up
operations in the rural areas, especially in the eastern part of Singapore, and
hundreds more Chinese were executed. All of them young and sturdy men who
could prove troublesome.[7]

The Japanese indulged in persecution of Chinese people after the
pying Singapore. Inevitably, Tan Kah Kee, the leader of the fund-
ing organization, became the target of the Japanese. Fortunately, Tan
escaped to Indonesia by boat prior to the arrival of the Japanese. Tan
k Sye (陈六使) was worried that nobody could take care of Tan, so had his
, Tan Eng Ghee (陈永义) follow Tan to Indonesia.[8] Tan Kah Kee might
been tortured or even killed if he had not escaped to Indonesia.

Before the Japanese army occupied Singapore, the British had destroyed
teries, generators and military vehicles on Tekong Island.[9] Residents of
island were terrified by the roar of guns and panicked because the British
y started to retreat. Resident Wong Kwong Sheng (黄光盛) described the
ation:

In 1941, Japanese army first came to Singapore and threw a bomb. We knew it.
Somebody said, "Japanese came to Singapore! Bomb!" Some houses on Robinson
Road were bombarded. At the night after three to four days, Kampong Permatang
was also the target of a bomb. But the bomb was too weak and missed its target,
going to the sea. In Kampong Selabin, we heard that Japanese were coming and
throwing bombs. We did not resist. It's like we can only wait to die. Nothing can
be done about it. At that time, the transportation was not convenient, unlike
nowadays.[10]

e, KY (2006). *The Singapore Story: Memoirs of Lee Kuan Yew.* pp. 57–58. Singapore:
gapore Press Holdings.
al History Interview with Lim Soo Gan (1982). Singapore: Oral History Department; *Pedigree
Chen in Chimei,* modified by Chen, JX (陈厥祥) (1963). *The Chronology of Chimei.* p. 122.
g Kong: Jue Xiang Chen.
al History Interview with Leong Teng Chit (1982). Singapore: Oral History Department.
ral History Interview with Wong Kwong Sheng (1982). Singapore: Oral History Department.

During the period between the retreat of the British and the arrival of t
Japanese, the islanders became mentally well prepared. According to resid(
Leong Teng Chit's (梁定哲) description, "After the British abandoned t
island, they left sugar, rice, cookies and cloth canopy. Bikes and scoot(
were taken by other residents and cloth canopies were modified as cloth(
Munitions, soldiers' clothes and food were buried."[11]

Prior to Japanese arrival on Tekong Island, women and children w(
sheltered in the forest, while men pernoctated at the intersection of roa(
to guard in case the Japanese entered the island. Members of the fun(
raising organization, at the same time, burnt all related documents to prot(
themselves from being persecuted by Japanese.[12] Some residents even ma(
a flag with the slogan "Long Live Japan" and hung it in front of the hous(
and prayed for their safety.[13]

One week after the Japanese occupied Singapore, they entered Teko(
Island and brought it under their control. Ng Kia Cheu recalled, "Japane(
came here. All people were called ... in front of the coffee shop (in Kampo(
Selabin), standing for three, even more than four hours. They were tann(
under the burning sun. Then the Japanese soldiers could not find anything to (
and asked those people to leave."[14] The Japanese army did not slaughter peop(
on Tekong Island possibly because of the following reasons. First, the Mala(
did not blow the whistle on the anti-Japanese movement of the Chinese (
Tekong Island. Second, there were not enough economic and human resourc(
on Tekong Island to support the fighting against Japan. Third, the brick fa(
tory owned by Tan Kah Kee was managed by a Taiwanese who could spe(
Japanese. The manager of the factory and Yang Yong Chang (杨永昌), who ha(
studied in Japan and was the founder of Eng Wah School, guaranteed to th(
Japanese that the islanders were not anti-Japanese, so they escaped from bein(
persecuted.[15] As Tekong Island was not essential to the economy or military,
was garrisoned by only 50 Japanese soldiers a month.[16]

As soon as the Japanese army occupied Tekong Island, Penghulu Tengk(
Ahmad was asked to gather all residents in military camp and was assigne(
by Japanese as the head the village with a three-flower medal of honor. She(
Mu Cun (沈木存) was also awarded a two-flower medal and was selected a(
the leader of the Chinese. Among the Malays, dozens of people were chose(

---

[11] *Oral History Interview with Leong Teng Chit* (1982). Singapore: Oral History Department.
[12] *Oral History Interview with Chin Sit Har* (1987). Singapore: Oral History Department.
[13] *Oral History Interview with Heng Siew Leng* (1982). Singapore: Oral History Department.
[14] *Oral History Interview with Ng Kia Cheu* (1982). Singapore: Oral History Department.
[15] *Oral History Interview with Wong Kwong Sheng* (2007). Singapore: Tekong Island Project; *Or(
History Interview with Wang Shou Qing* (2007). Singapore: Tekong Island Project; *History Intervie(
with Loo Geuang Fiyau* (2007). Singapore: Tekong Island Project.
[16] *Oral History Interview with Leong Teng Chit* (1982). Singapore: Oral History Department.

awarded one-flower medal. These chosen people were responsible for the
·eying Japanese's orders and mobilizing residents.[17] During the period of
ipation of the island by the Japanese army, men were require to remove
vay lines and pick up bullets and metal, which were carried away by boat
he Japanese. Former residents revealed that they had to search for water
food. Residents worked seven days a week, from 7.00 am to 12.00 pm,
ed for one hour, and again worked from 1.00 pm to 5.00 pm. Their salary
meager, about ten dollars of "banana bill."[18] Workers could also receive
, sugar and coffee powder every Friday.[19]

The Japanese gradually stabilized Tekong Island's situation and brought
nse of normalcy to the residents' lives. However, the Japanese did not
·rove people's lives but rather made them miserable. The Pacific War had
austed the Japanese army in China, and resources were fast diminishing.
·ng Teng Chit described the situation, "the payment stopped and the
lity of rice, sugar and coffee powder was poor."[20] In addition to collecting
al, some residents were assigned to cut trees in rubber plantations. The
·ays were required to pluck coconut, cook coconut oil and make *Attap*
·es.[21] At the end of the war, the Tekong Island residents were in serious
ncial trouble due to lack of goods and materials. To make a living, they
· farmed, went fishing and did business such as trading rice and fish,
iddition to working for the Japanese.[22] The banana bill printed by the
·anese had no value as there were not enough materials to support the
ie of the bill. Moreover, the difficulties of the war forced Japan to demand
·e goods and materials from the occupied areas. Accordingly, the price
·ood, oil and other products in Singapore rocketed.[23] The residents on
·ong Island were in a bad plight, so they had to barter or trade materials
he black market for a living.

In 1945, World War II was approaching the end. Germany uncondition-
· surrendered on 8 May. On 26 July, China, US and UK urged Japan
·urrender as soon as possible but the Japanese government rejected the
·nand. In order to end the war, the United States dropped the first atomic
·nb on the Japanese city of Hiroshima on 6 August 1945 and the second

---

·ral History Interview with Leong Teng Chit (1982). Singapore: Oral History Department; Oral
·ory Interview with Ng Kia Cheu (1982). Singapore: Oral History Department; Oral History
·rview with Wong Kwong Sheng (2007). Singapore: Tekong Island Project.
he bill was called banana bill as it was printed with a picture of banana.
·ral History Interview with Abdullab bin Ahmad (1984). Singapore: Oral History Department.
·ral History Interview with Leong Teng Chit (1982). Singapore: Oral History Department.
ttap is Malay name for a palm species and is categorized under the Palmae family.
·ral History Interview with Wong Kwong Sheng (2007) Singapore: Tekong Island Project; Oral
·ory Interview with Leong Teng Chit (1982). Singapore: Oral History Department; Oral History
·rview with Abu Samab bin Awang (1987). Singapore: Oral History Department.
ee, YM (1998). The Independence of Singapore. p. 32. Singapore: National Heritage Board.

bomb on Nagasaki on 9 August 1945. In Nagasaki, nearly 60% of the bui
ings were destroyed and the death toll reached 86,000 people, accounti
for 37% of the city's population. The bombs forced the Japanese forces
capitulate and unconditionally surrender on 15 August. On 2 Septemb
1945, Japan signed the surrender documents, effectively ending World W
II. The bombardment of Hiroshima and Nagasaki forced the Japanese
experience the disaster brought by imperialism. After defeat, Japan le
Singapore and the British returned to govern the island. Singapore was st
ruled by the colonial government after the war. Section 4.2 investigates t
influence of the British on Tekong Island.

4.2. Tekong Island Under British Government and Self-Governance

After World War II, the prevailing international situation deeply influence
people under colonial rule. Countries were divided in a dichotomous wa
the capitalist bloc, including the US and some countries of western Europ
founded the North Atlantic Treaty Organization, while the communi
bloc, including countries such as Soviet Union, Poland, Czechoslovaki
Hungary, Romania, Bulgaria, East Germany, Yugoslavia and Albania, esta
lished the Warsaw Treaty Organization. Two opposing political, econom
and diplomatic systems existed in Europe at the same time, giving ri
to Cold War. Two powers were in fierce competition in Asia as we
As soon as World War II ended, Kuomintang (supported by US) ar
the Chinese Communist Party (supported by Soviet Union) engaged in
power struggle in mainland China. On 1 October 1949, Communist force
eventually emerged victorious and established the People's Republic e
China. Communism hence extended further to Asia. For the purpose e
tempering the spread of communism, US, along with other nations in Europe
Asia and America, adopted containment measures on communist countrie
    The international situation inevitably affected the political situation i
Southeast Asia. After World War II, most regions of southeastern Asia wer
still colonies but the colonial countries' power was badly threatened due t
Pacific War. The victory of the Chinese Communist Party inspired colonie
striving for independence by force and brought colonial government to
tough test. The idea of left-wing politics had spread among Chinese i
the Singapore and Malaysia prior to World War II.[24] Later, the Malaya

---

[24]Chinese Communist Party had been propagating communism in Malaysia and other areas sinc
1924. See Gwee, HA (1966). *The Emergency in Malaya.* p. 1. Penang: Sinaran Brothers Limitec
in 1926, Communist Youth League was established in Singapore. Communists propagandize

munist Party was established in the April of 1930.[25] During the period
ghting against Japanese, those involved in Singapore and Malaya mainly
prised Chinese who organized the Malayan People's Anti-Japanese
y. Many of the members of the organization were Malayan communists.[26]
organization was secretly supported by the British government and
me stronger during the time when Japanese occupied Singapore and
aya. Japanese withdrew from these regions after they surrendered on
ugust 1945, and the British army entered Singapore on 5 September.
nwhile, during the two weeks interval, the Malayan communists started
apture traitors and made their identity public. After the Japanese left
ong Island, there were more than 50 anti-Japanese activists (both men
women) wearing military uniforms. They constructed a stage and hung
d flag in Kampong Selabin, claiming that the Japanese had surrendered
hem. These people replaced the national flag of Republic of China with
; of Malayan communists and celebrated the defeat of the Japanese.[27]
Malayan communists grew stronger after the end of World War II[28] but
e not recognized by the returning British government. They launched
rrilla operations, known as Malayan Emergency, to force the British
of Malaya.[29] Because of this threat, the colonial government was
tile to communists. After 1949, the British government tightened its
s on migration and severed contact between the Chinese societies in
gapore and Malaya and that in China.[30] At same time, Singapore was
arated from Malaya as an independent political entity. It seemed that
government was worried that the unification of Chinese would harm

ents at night schools and Chinese schools and had great influence on them. See Hanrahan, GZ
4). *The Communist Struggle in Malaya.* p. 8. New York: Institute of Pacific Relations.
hoo, KK (1984). Gerakan Komunis di Tanah Melayu Sehingga Tertubuhnya PKM. In *Darurat
3–1960,* Khoo, KK and HJ Nawang Adnan (eds.), p. 25. Kuala Lumpur: Muzium Angkatan
era.
verseas Chinese Association (新马侨友会) in Singapore and Malaysia (ed.) (1992). *Malayan
i-Japanese Army.* pp. 14–17. Hong Kong: Hong Kong Testimonies Publishing.
ral History Interview with Leong Teng Chit* (1982). Singapore: Oral History Department; *Oral
ory Interview with Heng Siew Leng* (1982). Singapore: Oral History Department.
alayan communists did not know guerila warfare before World War II but the British colonial
rnment encouraged communists to organize guerillas to fight against the Japanese. After Japan
endered, Malayan communists acquired large caches of deserted weapons, ammunitions and
l and thus strengthened their force. See Han, SY (韩山元) and Li, YL (李永乐), *Introduction
Malayan Communist during the War, Secret of Malayan Communist.* pp. 22–23. Singapore:
g Lee Publishers Pte Ltd.
ngkili, JP (1984). Darurat dan British, 1948–1960: Suatu Pernilaian. In *Darurat 1948–1960
o, KK and HJ Nawang Adnan (eds.), pp. 5–9. Kuala Lumpur: Muzium Angkatan Tenrera.
n 30 September 1951, Singapore and Malaya severed diplomatic relations with China. After
t, nobody was able to return to Singapore and Malaya from China. See *Nanyang Siang Pau
gapore),* 1 July 1951.

Malays' political rights and interests.[31] In fact, the colonial governme
was preventing communism from penetrating the Chinese and snatchi
the reign. The British were concerned about Chinese education, which w
thought to be influenced by communism and therefore become a tool
propaganda, so they strictly controlled the situation.

In addition to the threat from communists, the British government h
to face collapse of public faith on this once-strongest country in the wor
as the British were defeated by the Japanese. People's demand for the e
of colonial rule and for self-governance was growing, forcing the British
adjust its policy. From 1948 to 1959, the colonial government gradua
lessened its domination on politics. The first election in Singapore was held
1948 but only 6 of 22 seats in Legislative Council were open. In 1955, the fi
general election was held (to elect only 25 members of parliament, as near
half were appointed by the government) and led Singapore to semi–se
governance. In the election, the Labor Front won 10 seats and invited Baris
Nasional (also known as the Alliance)[32] in Malay Peninsula for organizing
united government. The leader of Labor Front, David Marshall, won and th
became the first Chief Minister of Singapore. A self-governance agreeme
was signed in May 1958. Elections were then held in May 1959, with t
People's Action Party winning 43 of 51 seats.[33] Secretary General Lee Ku
Yew was sworn in as the prime minister and Yusof Bin Ishak as the preside
of the Singapore.

Though drastic political change occurred in Singapore, it seemed th
Tekong Island was not influenced that much. To residents of the islan
Japanese withdrew, and the reoccupation of the colonial government broug
them stability in the price of commodities and living and good publ
security. Former resident Wong Kwong Sheng described the post-wa

---

[31]Tregonning, KG (1966). *Malaysia and Singapore.* pp. 35–36. Singapore: Donald Moor
Simandjuntak, B (1985). *Federalisme Tanab Melayu 1945–1963.* p. 60. Petaling Jaya: Penerb
Fajar Bakti.
[32]The Alliance comprised UMNO, Malayan Chinese Association and Malaysian Indian Congre
(MIC). The founder of UMNO (United Malays National Organization) was Datuk Onn Jaafa
who was a nobleman in Johor. It was formed by a series of Malay congresses in opposition t
Malayan Union. UMNO was not only the biggest in the Alliance but also the most powerful
Malaysia. Malayan Chinese Association (MCA) was a political party in Malaysia. It was formed b
Tan Cheng Lock (陈祯禄) to correspond to the emergency in 1949 with support from post-Wor
War II British Reoccupation Authority. At first, MCA was only an organization of welfare and wa
not transformed to a political party until 1951. MIC was constructed in 1946, positioning itself f
representation on behalf of the Indian community in the country. It has been one of ruling parti
in Malaysia since it joined the Alliance in October 1954.
[33]Among the candidates in People's Action Party, 34 were Chinese, 10 were Malays, 6 were India
and 1 was Eurasian. See Lee, KY (2006). *The Singapore Story: Memoirs of Lee Kuan Yew.* p. 29
Singapore: Singapore Press Holdings.

"we were satisfied with the public security. Everybody were fed. We
to Singapore to buy commodities and food. Time went by and the
d became prosperous."[34] Tekong Island was free from the political storm
blew during the general election in 1959 for self-governance. This island
nged to the constituency of Changi (樟宜). Candidates went to the island
romote themselves, posting their election posters and holding rallies for
icity. Candidates accompanied by leaders of Hakka and Chaozhouese
visited each household to garner votes.

In the 1950s, this small island developed rapidly due to construction
vities of the colonial government. A wharf was established and roads
paved. The first private electricity-generating station was constructed
ife became more convenient for residents.[35] On the other hand, the
nial government implemented a state of emergency, which brought in
migrants to Tekong Island. These migrants were Hakka mainly coming
Kulai[36] in Johor in southern Malaya. They wanted to go south to
ong Island because they were not willing to move to a new village.[37] The
ka from Johor made their living by practicing agriculture and animal
bandry, such as planting rubber, pineapples and vegetables and raising
. Their agricultural skills had greatly improved and were carried over by
migrants to Tekong Island, including extracting water and shoveling soil
g machines. The Tekong residents were impressed with these skills.[38] It
unexpected that the colonial authorities' policy on Malayan communists
not influence Tekong Island but instead lead to new migrants.

Post-war change occurred not only in politics but also in the society of
gapore. In the 1950s, there were many student and labor movements.
that time, the Singapore Federation of Trade Union instigated a strike
all industries. The strike at the Hock Lee Amalgamated Bus Company

---

ral History Interview with Wong Kwong Sheng (2007). Singapore: Oral History Department.
ral History Interview with Ng Boon Tiang (1982). Singapore: Oral History Department.
akka migrated along Johor River, Johor Strait and Straits of Malacca to Kulai to make a
   g. The Hakka included those from Huizhou, Hoshan, Jiaying Zhou, Dapu, Chixi, Fengshun
   Tongwan. They moved to Kulai, respectively, from Kuala Lumpur, Melaka and Singapore.
   HR (安煥然) and Liu, LJ (刘丽晶) (2007) (eds.) *Migration and Exploitation of Hakka from
   or.* p. 77. Johor Bahru: South Academy Publishing, Johor Bahru Hakka Association.
he British government had military cooperation with Malayan communists in order to defeat
   anese but their negotiation failed after World War II. The Anti-Japanese army went back to
   st and fought against the colonial authorities, which hence announced Malayan communists as
   al and declared a state of emergency. With a view of coping with the communists, the British
   menced relocation, also known as "New Villages." The plan aimed to force people move into
   villages constructed by the authorities and Chinese living in the country were thus forced to
   ndon their homes. New villages were surrounded by high barbed wire fences and guarded by
   ce day and night. People were in surveillance and totally had no freedom as if they were living
   concentration camp.
ral History Interview with Ng Boon Tiang (1982). Singapore: Oral History Department.

even caused riots. The society was thus in turbulence because of su~
demonstrations. At the same time, Nanyang University was establishe
which was very significant to the Chinese in Singapore, even in Southea
Asia. As Tan Lark Sye, the chairman of Fujian Association, was aware
the plight of Chinese education,[39] he proposed in the association's th~
committee assembly of 10th anniversary that the Chinese should constru
their own university.

The university was named "Nanyang University" by leaders from diffe
ent fields after a discussion on 20 February 1953.[40] Two major newspape~
Nanyang Siang Pau (南洋商报) and Sin Chew Jit Poh (星洲日报), express
their support to the construction of the university.

Tekong Island was not influenced by the student and labor movemen~
but the residents on the island were receptive toward Tan Lark Sye's plan
constructing a university. People supported the construction of the universi
in action when the students arrived on the island for fund raising. Mc
islanders were of middle or lower class and did not own a fortune. Ho~
ever, they contributed to the development of Chinese education, providi~
assistance to this landmark event along with the Chinese in Singapore.

Singapore had encountered drastic change during the period from Wor
War II to the election for self-governance in 1959. It seemed that Tekor
Island was not totally out of the picture. Islanders had suffered for thr~
years during the occupation of Japanese; the battle between communis~
and the British government brought the island some migrants (from Johor
the political and social change inevitably had an impact on the residen~
of the island. In 1960, Singapore began to face ethnic issues despite sel
governance. Internal and external political issues and future developmer
were challenges to Singapore. Section 4.3 explores the above issues and the
influence on Tekong Island.

4.3. The 1960s: A Period of Change

Two major events took place in the 1960s. On 16 September 1963, Singapor
joined the Federation of Malaysia but the Malaysian government declare
that Singapore was no longer one of the states of Malaysia on 9 August 196~
Singapore was thus forced to be independent. The Singapore populatio~

---

[39]Chinese courses in Singapore covered only from primary school to senior high school. Student
who wanted to study further needed go to China. Due to the communists' expansion, wester
countries adopted containment so people in Singapore were not allowed to go to China. Accordingl~
students were thus not able to study further.
[40]*Nanyang Siang Pau* (Singapore), 21 February 1953.

essively experienced joy and misery as the joining the federation of aysia offered Singapore large hinterland and potential future but the er event led the country to face an unpredictable future. During this od, internal problems, such as the conflict between right and left wing ethnic issues and external pressure were oppressing Singapore. Tekong id could not be free from the impact.

This section first probes into the mergence of Singapore and Malaysia. e the victory in the 1959 election, the People's Action Party had eavored in the mergence of these two regions. With an eye at uniting apore and Malaysia, the then Secretary-General Lee Kuan Yew tried ersuade the then Malaysian Prime Minister Tunku Abdul Rahman, who unwilling to promote the merger. He was worried that the Malay's regime ld be affected as Chinese outnumbered Malays. Lee also understood ku Abdul Rahman's concern that "every Chinese was a potential com- ist supporter."[41] Hence, Lee proposed the formation of a "federation" to ress the loyalty and diminish the Malay leader's suspicion and worry. The ration aimed to include the three annexed British territories in Borneo bah, Sarawak and Brunei), along with Singapore, into a federation so t the number of other ethnic groups would not threaten the position of ays. The British was also in support of Lee's suggestion and aggressively uaded Tunku Abdul Rahman. On 27 May 1961, Tunku Abdul Rahman l in public gathering, "Malaya is supposed to have mutual understanding h people in the British, Singapore, northern Borneo, Brunei and Sarawak ner or later. The time is not ripe. I can't say how to be understood but we d to proceed toward the goal and to consider carrying out the plan. These as should be merged together for political and economical cooperation."[42] Singapore was an independent country, the communists could exploit pholes to take over its regime, which directly affected Malaysia's security. is might be the reason of Tunku Abdul Rahman's transformation of his itude toward the mergence. After considering the pros and cons, Tunku dul Rahman and his consultants, Abdul Razak bin Haji Daro' Hussein Haj and Ismail Abdul Rahman, chose to include Singapore in Malaysia prevent the communists from growing stronger.

The path to the merging of the federation was fraught with obstacles. nic contradictions existed in Singapore and Malaysia; senior officials in gapore and Borneo held different opinions over the rule of the country; addition, the intervention of the left wing in Singapore and external

---

ee, KY (2006). *The Singapore Story: Memoirs of Lee Kuan Yew.* p. 426. Singapore: Singapore ss Holdings.
anyang Siang Pau (Singapore), 28 May 1961.

forces all made the merger more complicated. From 1961 to 1963, t
British held several rounds of negotiations with Tunku Abdul Rahman a
Lee Kuan Yew. Even though the two sides had many opposing points
view, they finally chose to give in after two years of negotiations. On
September 1963, Malaysia was formed. Tekong Island was not influenced
the political turbulence and its residents led their lives as usual. To peop
on the island, 16 September 1963 was just a day when their ruler chang
from the British to Malay. However, this significant event was followed
potential crises that affected Tekong Island. Besides the leaders' differi
opinions, neighboring countries such as Indonesia and Philippines express
their objections. On 16 September, Indonesia severed diplomatic relatio
with Malaysia and crowds gathered in front of the Malaysian and Briti
embassies, showing their dissatisfaction. In Kuala Lumpur, Malaysians al
gathered in front of the Indonesian embassy, throwing stones and burnii
the portrait of Indonesian president Sukarno to convey their displeasuu
In 1964, Indonesian agents landed on Johor in the south of the peninsu
to threaten Malaysian authorities.[43] Indonesia's shock action worried tl
residents on Tekong Island, who were concerned that there might be a
unexpected attack anytime.[44]

    Leaders in Singapore and Malaysia held different opinions over mai
issues. Singapore required the right to detain members of illegal organizatic
without trial according to the temporary provisions of the criminal la
In order to prevent communists in Singapore from applying for Malaysia
citizenship, the concerned authorities asked for an amendment to lim
Singapore citizens' entrance to Malaysia. Singapore thus responded by worl
ing to prohibit Malaysians from entering Singapore. Moreover, Singapo
requested for the provision of an Attorney General of the State, who cou
prosecute people on the basis of related laws in order to prevent corruptio
Nevertheless, Tunku Abdul Rahman was unwilling to give in to Singapore
demands. Lee Kuan Yew strategically strived for British support and sai
"The British were with me, and the pressure I applied through them worke
By 7 September, the Malayan Attorney-General and Razak between thei
had endorsed all the items in question except the delegation to Singapore c
the right to detain secret society gangsters. They did not want this to be i
the constitution and I had to be content with a simple letter of authority."[4]

[43]Lee, YM (1998). *The Independence of Singapore*. pp. 73–74. Singapore: National Heritage Boar
[44]*Oral History Interview with Huang Bing Song (黄炳松)* (2007). Singapore: Tekong Islan
Project; *Oral History Interview with Lea Guan Chong* (2007). Singapore: Tekong Island Projec
[45]Lee, KY (2006). *The Singapore Story: Memoirs of Lee Kuan Yew*. p. 503. Singapore: Singapo
Press Holdings.

apore's victory in the negotiation, however, contributed to a negative
lt. Lee Kuan Yew thus caused other officials' displeasure although Tunku
ul Rahman's authorities did not have much power. Lee said, "The Tunku
Razak were confirmed in their view that I was a difficult man to handle,
from then on they would always be guarded when dealing with me."[46]
r Malaysia was formed, there were still political battles taking place
he dark. The central authorities had tried to influence Singapore and
ated People's Action Party to replace its ruling position in Singapore.
election held in Singapore a few days after the mergence made Tunku
ul Rahman feel threatened by People's Action Party.
The election held on 21 September 1963 was significant to People's
ion Party for it won 37 seats among 51 while its opponent, Barisan
alis, won only 13 seats. The last one seat was taken by People's Unity
ty.[47] This landslide victory consolidated the position of People's Action
ty and broke left wing's stronghold in Singapore. It won the support
ost Chinese and the confidence of Malaysians as well. People's Action
ty's victory in the three constituencies,[48] where Malaysians accounted for
ority of the population, denoted the fact that it had won support from
erent ethnic groups. Tunku Abdul Rahman had wished to divvy People's
ion Party's political territory by Singapore Alliance consisting of UMNO,
ayan Chinese Association, MIC and Singapore People's Alliance led by
Yew Hock. However, his planning turned to be a failure. Singapore
ance failed to win even 1 of the available 42 seats.
Due to Singapore Alliance's failure, the authorities were aware of People's
ion Party's competence. UMNO was even displeased that PAP was
ported by different ethnic groups. If the trend extended to Malay
insula, the position of UMNO might be threatened. Accordingly, UMNO
ointed its Secretary-General Syed Ja'afar Albar as the "pioneer" for a
nterattack. Lee Kuan Yew once described Syed Ja'afar Albar:

Syed Ja'afar Albar was the hatchet man of the UMNO leaders hostile to
Singapore. Originally from Indonesia but of Arab descent, he was small, balding,
a bundle of energy with a round face, a moustache and a good, strong voice . . . he
was a great rabble-rouser, skilful in working up the mob and, as I was to learn,
totally ruthless and unscrupulous in his methods.[49]

---

ee, KY (2006). *The Singapore Story: Memoirs of Lee Kuan Yew.* p. 503. Singapore: Singapore
ss Holdings.
anyang Siang Pau (Singapore), 23 September 1963.
hree constituencies were South Islands, Kampong Kembangan and Geylang Serai.
ee, KY (2006). *The Singapore Story: Memoirs of Lee Kuan Yew.* p. 551. Singapore: Singapore
ss Holdings.

Syed Ja'afar Albar kept smearing People's Action Party, claiming th
the former was anti-Malay. He also criticized that, through Utusan Melayu
the party was inclined to favor some ethnic groups in order to prove
racial tensions. Utusan Melayu pointed that Malays were worried about t
distribution of stalls in the market in Geylang Serai and Malay educatio
falling behind because of PAP's policy. Syed Ja'afar Albar blamed PAI
victory in the three constituencies for using despicable methods.[51] T
purpose of UMNO and pro-UMNO press was to turn themselves into
defender of Malaysian group and to trigger ethnic awareness of Malaysia
in Singapore.

During the colonial period, different ethnic groups were separate
and ruled but chronic separation caused suspicion and misunderstandi
between these groups. The independence and the withdrawal of the coloni
government referred to the shift of power; nevertheless, ethnic problems we
not solved. The ethnic relationship between Singapore and Malaysia was ve
weak and the politicos took advantage of this for their own good. The ga
between ethnic groups was manipulated by politicos and the press, resulti
in the simmering of tensions between Chinese and Malays. In March 196
PAP decided to contest the state elections in Malaysia, which displease
UMNO. In the election in 1964, the Alliance won landslide victory, takir
89 seats (there were 104 seats in the parliament of Malay Peninsula)[52] whi
only C. V. Devan Nair from PAP took the seat in Bangsar.[53] Though th
Alliance emerged victorious in the election, it did not mean that UMNO
dissatisfaction over PAP's challenge was reduced.

After the state election in 1964, UMNO's movement against PA
proceeded and became more violent. The attack from UMNO and the pre
was recorded in Lee Kuan Yew's book:

> On 23 May, an editorial in the Utusan accused the PAP and me of inciting
> non-Malays to demand the abolition of the special rights of the Malays. On
> 11 June, the paper proclaimed, "Singapore UMNO directed to take steps to
> save PAP victims." The next day, another headline "Malays in Singapore today
> facing threat, pressure and oppression by the government. Do not treat the
> sons of the soil as stepchildren." A week later, the Utusan urged all Malays
> to "stand solidly behind UMNO in making strong and effective protests against
> the PAP government," and to call on Kuala Lumpur to take immediate action to
> protect their special rights. UMNO then published a "white paper" setting out

---

[50]Utusan Melayu was established in 1939 and was modified as Utusan Melaysia in 1967. See http://
forum-rencana-pmrsibu.blogspot.com/2008/09/sejarah-utusan-melayu-dan-duri-dalam.html
[51]Lee, KY (2006). *The Singapore Story: Memoirs of Lee Kuan Yew*, pp. 551–552. Singapor
Singapore Press Holdings.
[52]Milne, RS (1967). *Government and Politics in Malaysia*. p. 361. Boston: Houghton Mifflin.
[53]http://en.wikipedia.org/wiki/Malaysian-_general_election,_1964.

'in detail the sufferings of the Malays under the PAP led by Lee Kuan Yew."
Once more, they accused us of treating them as stepchildren, saying that the
Malays who were traitors to their own race and had voted for us were realizing
their mistake, because now the government intended to turn Geylang Serai into
another Chinatown.[54]

A branch of UMNO held an assembly of Malay and Muslim groups in
xing Theater (新星戏院) in Pasir Panjang on 12 July, listening to Malays'
vances, and to decide a way to cope up with the fate and plight of
Malays in Singapore.[55] The assembly had drawn 123 representatives
1 different Malayan groups and the Secretary-General of UMNO, Syed
far Albar, also attended the meeting. On the assembly, Syed Ja'afar
ar instigated Malayan groups with provoking words:

I am very happy today we Malays and Muslims in Singapore have shown unity
and are prepared to live or die together for our race and our future generation. If
there is unity no force in this world can trample us down, no force can humiliate
us, no force can belittle us. Not one Lee Kuan Yew, a thousand Lee Kuan
Yews... we finish them off... however much we are oppressed, however much
we are suppressed, however much our position has been twisted and turned by
the PAP government, according to Lee Kuan Yew's logic: Hey, shut up, you, you
minority race in this island. Here I say to Lee Kuan Yew: You shut up and don't
tell us to shut up.[56]

After the assembly, UMNO announced the creation of "Malay Operation
ncil" led by the parliament member Ahmad Haji Taff with 23 members,
organization aimed at striving for Malays' rights in Singapore.[57]
At the assembly on 12 July, the leader of UMNO called upon the
lay people to boycott talks to be held with PAP on 19 July. Although
appeal was sent via newspapers, the outcome was not effective. On
July, there were up to 83 Malayan representatives and 300 heads of
ages who attended the talks. Lee Kuan Yew stated to about 900 Malays
attendance that he would solve the problems of education, employment
l accommodation. The government promised to assist them and admitted
lays' special position; however, the Malays were not offered any privileges
it was regulated in the constitution in central government. The talks held
PAP were considered by UMNO as a tool to fragment the Malay society
Singapore. After these two meetings, the confronting positions of UMNO

---

ee, KY (2006). *The Singapore Story: Memoirs of Lee Kuan Yew*. p. 553. Singapore: Singapore
ss Holdings.
anyang Siang Pau (Singapore), 13 July 1964.
ee, KY (2006). *The Singapore Story: Memoirs of Lee Kuan Yew*. p. 554. Singapore: Singapore
ss Holdings.
anyang Siang Pau (Singapore), 20 July 1964.

and PAP were becoming clearer and more definite. It was a low-class ŀ
effective method for politicos to manipulate ethnic issues. As a result, t
relationship between ethnic groups worsened. This ethnic tension gave r
to bloody conflicts, which broke out on the birthday of Prophet Mohamm
on 21 July.

On 21 July 1964, the birthday of Prophet Mohammed, the Mala
in Singapore gathered in a vacant land in their town and walked ⋅
to Geylang Serai. They played the drums and chanted Al-Quran alo
on the way to celebrate the birthday. The Minister of Social Affai⋅
Othman bin Wok, and Malayan members in PAP also joined the gatherir
However, an Arabian attorney, Esa Almenoar, issued provoking words befo
departure stating, "Obviously, Allah wouldn't like Muslims to keep go⋅
relationship with non-Muslims. . . . Everything we do has to be controlled. ⋅
for those who intervened in our religion and expelled us from our hometow
Muslim said they are merciless and are doing evil things. . . . Enduran
and understanding would not help us tolerate internal or external peop
violating our castle, house and religion. . . . "[58] Before the parade, the crov
had been agitated, and some people clapped on the drums and kept yellir
along the road. At around 5.00 pm, while the procession approached Kallaﬞ
gas station, several young people left the crowd. One of the Chinese poli⋅
asked them in Malay to return to the procession and pushed one of the your
people who would not listen to the police's direction to join the crowd. Th⋅
behavior enraged others and about 20 Malays surrounded the policema⋅
threatening to assault him. At that time, two other police (a Chinese and
Malay) tried to rescue him from the siege but failed to calm down the crow⋅
The crowd went berserk and about 50 Malay people started to assault tl
Chinese police.[59]

The conflict in the parade contributed to the Malayan group's simmerir
rage. Some people in the parade even spread the rumor that Malays we⋅
attacked by the Chinese. This angered the Malays, who began to attac
the Chinese who were passing by and the nearby shops. Riots sequentiall⋅
occurred on many streets in Geylang Serai. As the news of riots sprea⋅
out, Chinese in other areas started to counterattack. The conflict betwee
Malays and Chinese extended to almost the whole of Singapore, includir
Queen Street, Victoria Street, North Bridge Road and Jalan Pasar.[60]

---

[58]Lau, A (1998). *A Moment of Anguish: Singapore in Malaysia and the Politics of Disengagemen⋅*
p. 163. Singapore: Times Academic Press.
[59]Lau, A (1998). *A Moment of Anguish: Singapore in Malaysia and the Politics of Disengagemen⋅*
p. 165. Singapore: Times Academic Press.
[60]Lau, A (1998). *A Moment of Anguish: Singapore in Malaysia and the Politics of Disengagemen⋅*
pp. 168–169. Singapore: Times Academic Press.

On the other hand, residents on Tekong Island were disturbed by the
in Singapore, and the whole island had an atmosphere of tension and
giving. Chinese residents figured out ways to protect themselves and their
lies. If something happened, folks alerted each other with firecrackers
that they could run to the rambutan orchard and hide inside until the
n.[61] In some families, members pernoctated in turn to be prepared for
emergencies.[62] A former resident said, "At that time, everybody was
ous. My grandfather bought a knife and iron to be prepared at home. My
tives organized a self-defense group. If anything happened, they informed
other by playing a gong and people would hide in the house of one of
relatives for one night until dawn."[63] The news of conflict in Singapore
ad to Tekong Island, so the Chinese and Malays were all on high
t and guarded themselves. For the purpose of preventing tragic events
n happening, Penghulu Tengku Ahmad invited representatives of Hakka,
ozhouese and Malays, convening a meeting in the community center of
npong Pahang. At the conference, Penghulu Tengku Ahmad stated that
ethnic groups had lived on the island for years and maintained a good
tionship and that people on Tekong Island should not be influenced by
t had happened in Singapore. Accordingly, he announced that Tekong
nd was no longer under martial law and that residents should to go back
eading their normal lives.[64]

As a result of the bloody conflict in Singapore on 21 July, the death
was up to 23, with 454 people injured.[65] Fortunately, a similar tragedy
not take place on Tekong Island. The reasons Tekong Island was able
endure the ethnic storm are as follows. First, residents were convinced of
ughulu Tengku Ahmad's decision.[66] Second, the Chinese and Malays on
kong had lived together for over a century. There was a profound and close
ationship between them. Third, there were no politicians on the island,
voking different ethnic groups. Compared to the peaceful Tekong Island,
pressure in Singapore was about to break out and another big storm was
proaching.

---

ral History Interview with Huang Chun Ying (2007). Singapore: Tekong Island Project.
ral History Interview with Hong Chu Lan (2007). Singapore: Tekong Island Project.
ral History Interview with Hong-Xia Guo (2007). Singapore: Tekong Island Project.
ral History Interview with Lea Guan Chong (2007). Singapore: Tekong Island Project.
ee, KC (李炯才) (1989). Pursuit of One's Country. p. 340. Taipei: Yuan-Liou Publishing.
enghulu Tengku Ahmad was fair and just in his rule and never favored any particular group.
refused to take bribes for helping others and even gave financial assistance to the poor.
refore, residents trusted and respected him. See Oral History Interview with Ng Boon Tiang
32). Singapore: Oral History Department; Oral History Interview with Huang Ming Xuan
07). Singapore: Tekong Island Project; Oral History Interview with Huang Sheng Jia (2007).
gapore: Tekong Island Project.

The ethnic conflict revealed the contradiction between PAP and UMN
In 1965, the competition of these two parties became fierce. First, Sing
pore Alliance was reorganized and Minister of Agriculture and Coope
tion, Mohamed Khir Johari, took over as chairman. Mohamed Khir Joh
announced to the press, "In the next election in 1967, the Singapore Allia
will win enough votes to organize the next government."[67] Obviously, t
Alliance was warning PAP, which showed no fear. As the way the extre
Malays used worried non-Malays in Malaysia, the concept of "Malaysian
Malaysia" proposed by Lee Kuan Yew was recognized by the non-Malay p
ties. Then, many parties, including People's Progressive party,[68] United Den
cratic Party in Penang,[69] Sarawak United People's Party,[70] United Nation
Kadazan Organization[71] and Party Machinda,[72] repeatedly contacted PA
After several rounds of negotiation, the four opposition parties (except Unit
National Kadazan Organization),[73] along with PAP, established the Malaysi
Solidarity Convention. Leaders of the five parties signed a pronouncemer
striving for the formation of Malaysian's Malaysia:

> A Malaysian's Malaysia means that the state is not identified with the supremacy,
> well-being and interests of any one particular community or race. A Malaysian
> Malaysia is the antithesis of a Malay Malaysia, a Chinese Malaysia, a Dayak
> Malaysia, an Indian Malaysia or Kadazan Malaysia and so on. The special and
> legitimate interests of different communities must be secured and promoted within
> the framework of the collective rights, interests and responsibilities of all races.
> The growing tendency among some leaders to make open appeals to communal
> chauvinism to win and hold their following has gradually led them also to what has
> been tantamount to a repudiation of the concept of a Malaysian Malaysia.... If
> people are discouraged and denounced for abandoning communal loyalties because
> they have found common ground for political action with Malaysians of other
> races, then the professed concern for a Malaysian Malaysia is open to serious
> doubts.[74]

---

[67]Lee, YM (1998). *The Independence of Singapore*. p. 89. Singapore: National Heritage Board.

[68]The former title of People's Progressive Party was Perak Progressive Party. It was establish
in Perak of Ipoh on 11 January 1953. Its title was changed to the present one in the March 195
The founders were Ceylon Tamil Attorneys, S. P. Seenivasagam and D. R. Seenivasagam, who we
brothers.

[69]In 1959, the second chairman of Malayan Chinese Association, Lim Chong Eu (林苍佑) disagre
with Tunku Abdul Rahman over the distribution of candidates' seat. After losing his position an
leaving UMNO, he founded United Democratic Party in Penang.

[70]Sarawak United People's Party was the first legal party in Sarawak and was greatly influenced k
socialism in early time. Most of the members were Chinese, and the party was supported by Iban.

[71]United National Kadazan Organization was the first party in Sabah which was founded on beha
of the non-Muslim aboriginals in Sabah. The founder Donald Stephens was a human rights activi
of Kadazan.

[72]The term "Machinda" refers to the union of three major ethnic groups in Sarawak: Malay, Chines
and Dayak. The party was a small local party comprised of non-Malay.

[73]Wang, GZ (1997). *Ethnic Politics in Malaysia 1955-1995*. p. 91. Taipei: Tangshan Publishing.

[74]Lee, KY (2006). *The Singapore Story: Memoirs of Lee Kuan Yew*. p. 605. Singapore: Singapor
Press Holdings.

The alliance of opposition parties and the proposal of "Malaysian's
aysia" gave the non-Malays hope but at the same time was a cause
/orry for the Malays. As different ethnic groups were in confronting
tions, their relationships had always been unstable. The Malays kept
sing Tunku Abdul Rahman to arrest Lee Kuan Yew, who was considered
danger to Malay interest. The political world was fraught with tension,
oth Tunku Abdul Rahman and Lee Kuan Yew were looking for a solution
he problem. It seemed that the separation of Singapore from Malaysia
one of the solutions. After several rounds of secret negotiations between
1 sides, it was decided to let Singapore be independent. Separation of
gapore and Malaysia seemed to be the best solution to end the bleeding
flict. Lee Kuan Yew was quoted as saying that:

At about noon on 7 August , I (Lee Kuan Yew) went to the Residency to see the
Tunku (Tunku Abdul Rahman) I waited for some 30 to 40 minutes in the sitting
room while he was conferring with some of his officials in the dining room-I could
see them in deep conversation through the glass door. Then he came out and
sat with me alone for about 40 minutes. I began, "We have spent years to bring
about Malaysia. The best part of my adult life was to work toward Malaysia, from
1954 to 1963. We have had only less than two years of Malaysia. Do you really
want to break it up? Don't you think it is wiser to go back to our original plan,
which the British stopped, a looser federation or a confederation?" But from his
body language, I knew the Tunku had made up his mind. He said, "No. I am past
that. There is no other way now. I have made up my mind; you go your way, we
go our own way. So long as you are in any way connected with us, we will find
it difficult to be friends because we are involved in your affairs and you will be
involved in ours. Tomorrow, when you are no longer in Malaysia and we are no
longer quarrelling either in parliament or in the constituencies, we'll be friends
again, and we'll need each other, and we'll cooperate."[75]

The separation of Singapore and Malaysia was imperative under the
vailing situation. The date of 9 August was significant to the separation.
Malaysia, representatives of lower house were requested to vote for the
of supporting the separation of Singapore and Malaysia and the bill was
proved on the day. In Singapore, Lee Kuan Yew announced to the people
ough television broadcasting that Singapore had become independent
m Malaysia. It can be seen from the television footage that the former
me Minister, Lee Kuan Yew, spoke with tears, "it is painful whenever
recalled the moment of signing the document. To me, it was a miserable
ment in my life. I had been proposing the merge of these two areas.
are connected geographically, economically and ethnically. . . . It's all
r."[76] The independence of Singapore was not the first alternative but

ee, KY (2006). *The Singapore Story: Memoirs of Lee Kuan Yew.* p. 640. Singapore: Singapore
ss Holdings.
ee, YM (1998). *The Independence of Singapore.* p. 102. Singapore: National Heritage Board.

was completed by compulsion. It was not joyful at all as the leader had face many problems such as unemployment and industrial development industry in Singapore.

As for Tekong Island, Singapore's exit influenced its business. Aft Changi Road was open to vehicular traffic, it gradually replaced the tra position of Tekong Island. When Singapore was in the Federation Malaysia, people in Johor and on Tekong Island had constant busine interactions; after Singapore's exit, people from Johor rarely went to Teko Island for business. The trade function of Kampong Selabin almost d appeared and stores closed down one by one. Thus the residents Tekong Island made their living only by agriculture and fishing. Meanwhi Singapore was experiencing drastic change and this had a great impact Tekong Island. The lives of Tekong island residents would also be influenc by this change.

4.4. Conclusion

In this section, the main goal is to explore the influence of Singapo on Tekong Island during World War II. Prior to the war, the Chinese Singapore aggressively supported the anti-Japanese movement, and a gre deal of financial assistance and material resources were donated to th Chinese army in combat zones. Though there were no wealthy businessme on Tekong Island, its residents also contributed even their small income save their motherland. It could be seen from the anti-Japanese moveme that Chinese on the island recognized their ethnicity. As the Chinese Tekong Island and Singapore migrated there in the late 19th century, to tho migrants, Mainland China was their hometown and mother country an Tekong Island was just a place to earn a livelihood. National consciousne urged them to support the movement against Japan. When Pacific W broke out, Singapore was not able to avoid the combat. In 1942, Japane invaded Singapore and killed many Chinese as retribution for their ant Japanese movement. In contrast, the Chinese on Tekong Island were fre from the persecution, thanks to the stable ethnic relationships and th poor but simple lives on the island. Nevertheless, during the period Japan's occupation, residents on the island had to work and provide goo and materials for the Japanese. Accordingly, islanders had lived in a environment short of material resources. In August 1945, US dropped atomi bombs on Japan and this event led to the end of Pacific War, with th Japanese unconditionally surrendering to the Allies. The British returned t Tekong Island, and the islanders' lives turned back to normal. As resident

he island celebrated the end of the war, ethnic conflicts in Singapore
: about to break out. While the colonial government was not capable of
;ing against Japan, the people of the colony started to advocate for their
ιtry's independence. The colonial authorities in Singapore were aware of
trend and began to use their power, trying to maintain their influence
ost-colonial times. Singapore went through a transition from semi–self-
:rnance to self-governance and later joined the Federation of Malaysia.
whole of Singapore was full of the atmosphere of anti-colonialism.
hermore, the battle of right and left wing and ethnic conflict cause
ιoil in the international politics, and this also affected Singapore. On
other hand, residents on Tekong Island, away from the political storm,
:ly felt the tension in Singapore and led their utopian lives as usual.
ause of the small population and outlying position, Tekong Island was
: to escape from the political storm and even the bleeding conflict between
ιese and Malays on 21 July 1964. From the above-mentioned incidents,
ɔuld be concluded that different ethnic groups living in the same space
1 to communicate with each other for mutual understanding. On Tekong
nd, Chinese and Malay had lived together for almost one century. They
)ed each other and had no communication gap since some of the Malays
.erstood Hakka or Chaozhou dialect and most Chinese also understood
ιay.[77] With deep mutual understanding, they were not easily provoked by
ticians, so there were no ethnic conflicts on the island. As the problem
ween Singapore and Malaysian governments was getting worse, Tunku
:lul Rahman sensed that he could not control the situation anymore and
: Kuan Yew was also aware of the seriousness. After several rounds of
otiations, the two leaders decided to make Singapore independent. On
ιugust 1965, Singapore declared its independence, and Tekong Island
; one of the places controlled by Singapore. With a small territory and
le resources, Singapore had to figure out ways to effectively manage and
·elop this little island, including Tekong Island. At the time, residents on
:ong Island celebrated their independence, their lives changed with the
·elopment of Singapore, which was not expected by the islanders. The next
ιpter probes into how the management and development of Singapore's
·nomy influenced Tekong Island and the residents' lives.

---

ral History Interview with Antung Lee (2007). Singapore: Tekong Island Project; *Oral History*
:rview with Lee Tong Soon* (2007). Singapore: Tekong Island Project.

CHAPTER 5

The Development of Tekong Island

9 August 1965, Singapore separated from Malaysia and became inde-
dent, which opened a new chapter in the history of the city state.
ever, Singapore, a small country with a population of 2 million, had
face problems concerning the economy, diplomacy, national defense
ethnicity. The major issue that People's Action Party (PAP) needed
ackle was the deteriorating economy. After Singapore separated from
aysia, the hostile attitude of neighboring countries worsened Singapore's
iomy and the unemployment rate continued to increase, endangering the
ntry's economy. Therefore, the government endeavored in developing the
iomy, and not relying on the other side of Johor–Singapore Causeway and
litional markets in the south. To stimulate its economy, the Singapore
ernment viewed the entire world as its marketplace. In order to fully
elop Singapore, the scheme included a master plan for the development
he economy, territory, education, etc. to empower people and enhance
global competitiveness. Tekong Island was hence influenced by these
elopments. Sections 5.1 and 5.2 investigate whether Tekong Island
sformed as a result of Singapore's development and the link between
nation's progress and the disappearance of Tekong Island's villages.

. Tekong Island Under Singapore's Development

e Singapore government had encouraged industrial development since its
aration from Malaysia to generate employment. The Dutch economist
Albert Winsemius suggested the authorities establish an Economic
velopment Board (EDB) to attract foreign capital by providing "one-
p management" solutions. EDB aimed to support industrial growth by
ivities such as providing financial assistance to corporations, clearing
d and building factories.[1] In addition to promoting industrialization and
ving problems between labor and capital for creating a better investment
ironment, the Singapore government also endeavored to create basic
rastructure such as expressways, well-connected roads, industrial zones,

---

e, YM (1998). *The Independence of Singapore.* p. 103. Singapore: National Heritage Board.

and residential areas. All these efforts bore fruition and enabled Singapor
economy to rapidly develop in the following two decades. Employme
opportunities thus drastically increased, and people's income also rc
quickly. For example, Singapore's GDP in 1960 was S$1,330 but climbed
S$12,290 in 1982, which is evidence of its astonishing growth.[2] In 1960s, t
unemployment rate was up to 10% but, in 1980s, an extra 150,000 forei
laborers were needed. Even now there is huge demand for foreign lab
These statistics show that Singapore did not collapse after the separati
but rather has kept consolidating its economic position in the world.

Last celebrations of the birth of "Tuan" held by residents of Tekong Island in 1986.

With the development of the economy, the government did not overloc
the problem of housing. In the 1950s, the housing environment in Singapo
was terrible so it had to be improved as part of economic development. Befo
PAP held power, it included the issue of people's housing in its politic
views. After emerging victorious in elections, PAP formed the Housing
Development Board in February 1960. The board planned the constructio
of large buildings, offering low-priced houses for many families. As a resul
many people could possess their own homes and the available land wa
utilized to its full play. As a result of the authorities' long-term impetus, 80
of the people in Singapore lived in the buildings planned by the governmen
Villages in the country gradually vanished.

---

[2]You, PS (游保生) and Lin, CY (林崇椰) (1984). (Eds.) *The Development of Singapore in the Pa
20 Years.* p. 279. Singapore: Nanyang Sin Chew Lianhe Zaobao.

While Singapore was developing, Tekong Island was not ignored. Prior ingapore's independence, the government established the Pulau Tekong munity Center in Kampong Pahang and Kampong Selabin Community er in Kampong Selabin, respectively, for the purpose of promoting cul- l and art activities and providing the islanders a place for entertainment. community centers offered residents places to get together and interact each other. Kampong Selabin Community Center even provided people learning opportunities. Community centers enriched people's lives worked as the best place for discussions, learning and holding parties so adually substituted the Chinese clan association.

As Tekong Island was about to progress, its residents' lives changed the development. In the early 1970s, the government announced the mandeering of lands with less population for military purposes, and ong residents did not object to the government's arrangement. An official and Authority, Lim Chin Joo (林清如), described the prevalent situation residents' attitude, "the agent of the authority reported the land's dition, vegetation and the number of residents. I confirmed the report he island and compensated residents for their loss according to related lations.... I went to the island every day for a whole month. People e were very friendly. They were neither hostile to me nor did they protest inst the requisition."[3] A Malay resident also recalled the situation and sense of dejection among the residents, "the government sent someone measure the land and houses. We could only wait and accept it. If we sted the arrangement, it's like a mouse or deer fighting an elephant. were not as powerful as the authorities."[4] After being compensated, the dents started to move out of the commandeered land. The military camp, ler the request from the member of parliament in Changi, also provided itary vehicles and ferryboats to assist in the residents' relocation. Some ved to Singapore while others chose to move to villages that were not nmandeered, such as Kampong Selabin. In the 1970s, the population on tong Island started to decrease because of the relocation.

Since the land was used for national defense, Tekong Island had both itary and civilian populations. Tekong Island further developed when NDEF installed a garrison. For example, in 1973, the committee of mpong Selabin Community Center requested the local residents and diers to pave an asphalt road from Kampong Selabin to the second mili- y camp in Kampong Sanyongkong; in 1979, the road was equipped with

---

anhe Zaobao (Singapore) 9 September 2007.
al History Interview with Abdullab bin Ahmad (1984). Singapore: Oral History Department.

streetlamps for army and residents' convenience and telephone lines were a
installed. The chairman of Singapore City & Country Advisory, Goh Ch
Chua (吴秋泉), led a team inspecting Tekong Island. The water supply a
roadways were improved[5] and the construction of reservoir and other roa
were also completed. Tekong Island hence had a brand new look and qual
of life also greatly improved. However, despite the development, the civili
population on the island was declining and the rising quality of life was n
able to retain people in the village. At that time, Chinese and Malay you
left for Singapore for further studies or work.

Further economic success continued through the 1980s and this amazi
growth made Singapore one of the "Four Asian Tigers" with respect
economic development, together with Taiwan, South Korea and Hong Kor
With rapid development, Singapore was in demand of land and talent. As t
biggest outlying island, Tekong Island was the next target for developmer
Section 5.2 researches the reason natural villages no longer exist on t
island, the affection between the residents and the island and how they fe
when leaving the island.

5.2. The Disappearance of Villages on Tekong Island

The biggest outlying island of Singapore, Tekong Island is surrounded by viridity.
Located in the north of Singapore, the island is quiet and beautiful. Streams pass
through and waves gently bob up and down. Tekong Island, with its lush cover of
flowers and grass, is the land of the islanders' birth, growth and dreams. Laughter,
anger, sadness and joy resonate here.[6]

The above text was quoted from the prologue of *Loved Teko*
(《恋念德光情》), whose author was Zou Chong Han (邹崇汉), a former reside
of Tekong Island. As Tekong island was the motherland of many people, the
had deep affection toward the land. However, due to economic developme
and the government's plan, people were force to leave the island. They we
left with only memories of their beloved island.

The rapid development of Singapore widened the gap between th
city and countryside, which seemed to be an inevitable part of progres
The attraction of the city lights proved irresistible, and people left the
hometowns to utilize the huge gamut of opportunities that Singapo
provided. This urban migration also did not spare Tekong Island. Accordin
to the census in 1957, the population on Tekong Island was 4,169[7] bu

---

[5]Ho, KF (1993). *History Pulau Tekong & Tian Kong Buddhist Temple.* p. 92, 106. Singapor
Ho, KF.
[6]Chong Han (1992). *Loved Tekong.* p. 1. Singapore: Changwu Publishing.
[7]*Report on the Census of Population 1957* (1964). p. 109. Singapore: Government Printer.

declined to $4,069^8$ in 1969, based upon the research conducted by the
artment of Geography of Nanyang University. The number dropped even
r to $2,600^9$ in 1980 because the islanders continued to move out for
e than 23 years. Agriculture and fishing were the main occupations of
islanders, and their income was quite low. There was also potential
nployment on the island because rubber tappers worked less than
lays a month, sailor 19 days and fisherman less than 20 days.^{10} This
pelled the youth to leave for Singapore in search of better opportunities.
the other hand, industries in Singapore kept growing, especially the
tronic industry, which started flourishing under PAP's support. The
ut of electronic appliances sharply increased and it became the third
or industry, behind chemical and petroleum industries. Textile and
iture industries also quickly developed. With the sustained efforts of
government and industries, Singapore's industrial products entered the
rnational market.^{11} After independence, Singapore's economy drastically
v, with simultaneous rise in job opportunities, so the Tekong Island
th made a beeline toward Singapore. Given the fact that Singapore
becoming industrialized, the countryside diminished and its economic
1e also declined. According to the statistics in 1980, the labor involved
griculture and fishing accounted for only 1.9% of the entire Singapore
or force.^{12}
Events such as the relocation of Tekong Island youth, the expropriation
lands for military purpose and the cessation of trade with Malaysia
r Singapore's independence had great impact on Tekong Island. The
ernment also decided not to encourage any residents on the island.
he 1970s, Tekong Island was planned as a military base and its residents
e encouraged to move to Singapore. In the 1980s, Singapore's prosperity
reased while that of Tekong Island was on the downturn. Islanders left
pursuing studies or in search of employment. The decreasing population
responded to the government's plan. In the early 1980s, as the authorities
nned to commandeer the land on Tekong Island, agents were sent to
nmunicate with the residents. During Chinese New Year, Teo Chong Tee

1, ZB (1971). *Population and Usage of Land on Tekong Island.* p. 8. Unpublished honors thesis,
yang University.

nsus of Population 1980 Singapore. p. 25. Singapore: Department of Statistics (1981).

Ju, ZB (1971). *Population and Usage of Land on Tekong Island,* p. 20. Unpublished honors
is, Nanyang University.

hoi, KK (崔贵强) (1994). *Chinese in Singapore — From A Trade Harbor to An Independent
ntry.* p. 263. Singapore: Singapore Federation of Chinese Clan Associations.

heng, LK (1985). *Social Change and the Chinese in Singapore.* pp. 90–99. Singapore: University
ss.

(张宗治), Parliament Secretary of Social Affairs and a parliament meml
in Changi area, visited residents on Tekong Island with other officials a
helped them move to Singapore. In order to pacify residents and notify th
of the purpose of the expropriation, Teo Chong Tee went deep into t
villages and tried to answer residents' questions, assisting people on how
apply for government housing.[13]

With the government's persuasion, communication and assistance, re
dents moved out of Tekong Island in succession. On 9 September 1986, t
last temple on the island, Tian Kong Buddhist Temple, was moved to Bed
North Avenue 4 in Singapore, which denoted the end of relocation. At th
time, only few households remained on the island. They were able to mo
to Singapore as soon as their new residences were ready.[14] The migration
residents on Tekong Island was completed in 1987, and the island has be
used as military training base since then.

The Tekong Island residents found it difficult to forget the island's fore
cover, sunsets, harbor, well in Kampong Selabin, vegetable farms, rivers a
simple lives they led. Even people living in Singapore were fond of taking
short trip to or camping at Tekong Island. Only when they were on the islar
could they enjoy the love of Mother Nature and recall their past on Tekor
Island. Nevertheless, the cities had been fully developed and the countrysi
would be the next target for development. The government chose the pa
of progression rather than leaving the countryside untouched. People ha
no alternative but to comply with the government's mandate and leave tl
land where they had spent half their lives.

Some residents from Tekong Island were not accustomed to living
Singapore as they considered the public housing too crowded, noisy ar
uneasy.[15] One of them said, "I couldn't get used to the life away from Tekor
Island. Just couldn't forget it. I had a dog when living on Tekong Island ar
it was a pity I couldn't bring it with me. If a stranger took something in tl
house, it would grip it and howl as if it was telling him not to take anythin
here. But he did not bite people."[16] Some people described their parent
situation, "When they just moved out of Tekong Island, they couldn't g
used to the life in Singapore at all. The space was large on Tekong Islanc
They planted vegetable and fruit for their own need. They were afraid c
venturing out of the public housing when they just moved in."[17] It too

---

[13] *Nanyang Siang Pau* (Singapore), 11 February 1982.
[14] *Lianhe Zaobao* (Singapore), 20 September 1986.
[15] *Oral History Interview with Abdullah bin Ahmad* (1984). Singapore: Oral History Departmen
[16] *Oral History Interview with Antung Lee* (2007). Singapore: Tekong Island Project.
[17] *Oral History Interview with Lee Tong Soon* (2007). Singapore: Tekong Island Project.

for those residents to get accustomed to the new life in Singapore. 1 though they could adjust themselves to the new environment, they cherished the memory of their life on Tekong Island. Lee Tong Soon, —mer resident of Tekong Island and now the chairman of Thai Village lings Ltd., stated, "I miss my hometown so much. If permitted, I would a land by the sea and live there."[18] I found, during the interview, that y residents of Tekong Island felt sad but could not help moving out of island.

As they missed their hometown very much even many years after the —ration, they figured out various ways to return to Tekong Island. One ae residents, Chen Ting Zhong, accompanied a friend's son, who went he island for military service, arriving on Tekong Island. Chen said, vent to the island with a friend whose son served in the military. But movement was restricted to some places so I couldn't go back to my old se. I feel so sad. It's hard for others to understand how I feel."[19] Another aer resident, Loo Geuang Choon, landed on Tekong Island for official iness saying, "When working for the Ministry of National Defense, at es I had the chance back to Tekong Island. For the past dozens of years, ent fishing near Tekong Island by a rented boat with my brother or er family members at leisure. We went around the island and took a look igh we could not step into the island."[20] Such behavior indicated how y missed the island. They all hoped Tekong Island would no longer be a itary base so that they could return to their hometown someday.

The Achievements of Former Residents of Tekong Island

ough the villages on Tekong Island are now part of history, the enterprising nders have contributed a lot to Singapore's development. Some of the standing citizens from Tekong Island are listed in this section.

Chee King (吴初庆)

rn in 1931, Ng Chee King had lived in the China until he was nine years , when he moved to Kampong Sanyongkong Parit on Pulau Tekong. had studied in a private elementary school until fourth grade. Like aer islanders, Ng had lived in an unstable environment under Japanese's :upation.

ral History Interview with Lee Tong Soon (2007). Singapore: Tekong Island Project.
ianhe Zaobao (Singapore), 9 September 2007.
ral History Interview with Lea Guan Chong (2007). Singapore: Tekong Island Project.

Ng moved to Kampong Selabin with his family after Singapore beca
independent. He purchased dried coconut and other local products fr
islanders and sold these products at the Tian-Cheng Grocery Store, wh
was founded by his parents. With their hard work and endeavor, the st
was expanded and was operated for 32 years. After 1977, the residents
the island gradually migrated to Singapore since the government planned
use Tekong Island for military purposes. At that time, Ng's father pass
away and his family chose to live in housing arranged by the government
Chai Chee Area. Though Ng, as well as his family, could no longer run th
store, he was invited by Xie (吴初庆), who had been working in the sa
industry, to sell local products, seafood and groceries in retail in Ng's t
stalls in Pasir Panjang Wholesale Center. Ng's was named as Soon Hup Se
Yong Kee Importer and Exporter (顺合成永记出进口商), which grew rapi
since Ng was familiar with the business in this industry and Singapor
economy developed drastically in the late 1970s. As Xie planned to expa
to other industries, the store was thus operated by Ng alone and the nar
was changed to Ng Say Seng (吴生成).

Although the business was located in a remote island, Ng strived ha
and embraced the change in environment. Now his sons and daughters ha
their own businesses. Ng and his wife can relax and travel around the wor
to enjoy their life because their grandsons will help them run the store wh
they are free on holidays.

Loo Geuang Fiyan (吕玩标中医师)

Loo was born in Pulau Tekong Kechil in 1941 and moved with his fami
to Kampong Selabin when he was 13 years old. He studied in Oi Wa
School and worked as a boatman's assistant on Pulau Tekong–Changi fer
after graduating in 1956. His job then was to collect the ferry fare an
take care of the passengers. During the Chinese New Year, one of tl
Singaporeans who worked in a pharmacy of Chinese herb introduced Lo
to the pharmacy in Joo Chiat Place as an apprentice. At that time, Loo ha
to deal with everything he was asked. Two years later, the pharmacy wa
moved to China Street. Loo was aware that Chinese Physicians Trainin
School (新加坡中医学校) was near the pharmacy so he registered for th
entrance exam with his friend. After the President You Xing Nan (游杏南
was informed that Loo did not graduate from high school, Iou gave Lo
two essay questions for him to choose one to answer. The first one was a
ancient saying, "Before the rest of the world starts worrying, the schola
worries; after the rest of the world rejoices, he rejoices," and the second on
was "What do you think regarding Chinese medicine." Loo chose the latte

-tion and succeeded the test to enter the school. Then, Loo worked during
ime and studied at night, completing the courses, and graduated in
. Soon Loo became one of the members in Chinese Medicine Association
师公会) and applied for the job as a volunteer teacher in Singapore
ng Hwa Medical Institution (中华医院). The next year, Loo went to its
ch in Geylang and started to work when it opened in July. Loo also
ed as a volunteer doctor in Serangoon and Toa Payoh branches at night.
inally working in the pharmacy, Loo transferred to another pharmacy
h purchased and sold medicine at wholesale prices. In the daytime, he
Chinese medicine; at night after 6 pm, he was a volunteer doctor in a
ital. During the period, he became a clinician at Singapore College of
litional Chinese Medicine and progressed to be a formal teacher in the
ge in 1973.

After he had gained some experience, Loo was determined to open his
lical institution in Everton Park in 1981, namely Yee Chang Medical
(益昌参茸药行). Because of public praise, the number of his patients
rising. Loo became a well-known physician of Chinese medicine in
apore. He was once the vice president of Chinese Medicine Association,
superintendent of Chung Hwa Medical Institution(中华医院) and the
ident of Singapore Chinese Medicine Union (中药公会).

Loo attributed his success to his motto, "Being diligent for progress."
m being a poor child without educational resources in remote area, he
ked hard to achieve success.

far Bin Kassim (耶亚华)

ar Bin Kassim was born in Tekong Island in 1943 and studied in Ai Hwa
ool. After graduating from Whompoa Secondary School, he went to
yang University and majored in Chinese, graduating as the first Malay
dent in 1971.

After graduation, he had worked in Majlis Ugama Islam Singapore
UIS), also known as the Islamic Religious Council of Singapore, which was
ablished as a statutory body in 1988. (see Chapter 3 for more information
Mr. Jaffar Bin Kasam).

Kiau Seng (何侨生)

was born in a small town in Southern Johore in 1945. When Ho's mother
s giving birth to him, there was nobody to assist in delivering the baby, so
used crushed glass bowl to cut off the umbilical cord. Ho had 14 siblings.
moved to Pulau Tekong Kechil with his family and studied at Pulau
kong Primary School. Ho later continued his education at Dunman High
ool. As a president of The Nanyang Khek Community Guild, Ho regarded

himself as not well-educated and an impoverished and introverted pers(
In retrospection, he says calmly, "One step at a time, one step at a time ..
Although Ho is not voluble, he is a humble and modest entrepreneur.

Singapore became independent in 1965, and it was a period of gr(
societal transformation. A city state, namely Singapore, without natu:
resources has to import even drinking water from Malaysia, but it tra:
formed into one of the Four Tigers in Asia by transshipment trade and forei_
investment. Ho started to work as a salesman in STORA, a Sweden-bas
steel corporation one year after Singapore became independent, promoti
special steel. Thought Ho entered this industry by accident, he learned
lot during the four years by delivering products and dealing with relat(
affairs at the The Port of Singapore Authority and the bank. In the 197(
very few people were aware of special steel. Products of special steel we
rare, not to mention salesmen in this field. Ho was not eloquent and co:
not speak Cantonese, which was widely used in the industry. He spar(
no effort learning this dialect, attempting to sell the products to eve
interested company. Unlike steel, selling special steel requires experti:
Ho envisaged the potential and market of special steel and his care
started to develop. Due to rapid development of modern industries, especial
shipping, navigation and national defense, the demand for special ste
started to increase.

At the age of 25 years (in 1970), Ho raised S\$10,000 and founded t}
Leong Jin Corporation Pte Ltd (隆英公司). At that time, a German-bas(
corporation was searching for a commercial agent in Southeast Asia, ar
learnt about Ho, who was an experienced salesman in special steel. Becau:
of Ho's specialty and honesty, the German corporation decided to consign tl
steel to Ho and allowed Ho to pay for the steel in installments without ar
collateral. There was no written contract but only faith and trust betwe(
the German corporation and Ho which led to this collaboration.

In 1975, STORA was determined to withdraw the capital in Singapo:
and move to Hong Kong and hoped that Leong Jin Corporation could tal
over the factories. Then Leong Jin Corporation consulted with the bank ar
took over STORA in installments.

Leong Jin Corporation grew rapidly and its revenue also increased ever
year. Then the products were exported to overseas markets, such as Malaysi:
In 1978, ThyssenKrupp AG, a well-known German-based steel corporatior
planned to expand its market to Asia and consigned its products to Leon
Jin. In the 1980s, Ho transferred the ownership of some of the shares t:
the dominant steel corporation. Leong Jin became one of the partners of
multinational corporation.

Though Ho had great achievements in his career, he has kept a low-profile without flaunting his accomplishments. He sequentially donated ⅰillion RMB to Huang Jin Town (黄金镇) in Feng Shun County, Guang-ℊ Province, China. The target of his donation included Huang Jin High ⅰol, the hospital, the reservoir, and scenic spots like Zhoung Hua Dragon ≜龙) and the statue of dripping Guanyin (滴水观音). As a descendent of ka in Feng Shun, Ho tried his best to pay back to the society.

As recent as 2008, Ho donated S$200,000 to College of Confucius, yang Technological University, and successfully held "Nanyang Chinese rature Award" on 22 November 2008. Former residents of Tekong Island ⅰding Ho, Chen Ting Lei (陈廷雷) and Lu He Nan (吕河南) also sponsored project. Ho was the former president of Foong Shoon Fui Kuan, the Pres-ⅰt of Fong Yun Thai Association, and the incumbent Vice President of ℊapore Federation of Chinese Clan Associations (新加坡宗总会馆联合会), was awarded the Public Service Medal by the President of Singapore in ⅉ.

Kok Chin Yon (郭镇莹医生)

Kok was born in 1949. His father, Kok Zi Yi (郭子翼), was the founder principal of Chung Foh School (中和学校) in Kampong Sanyongkong. Kok was in the English class when he studied in Pulau Tekong Primary ⅰool and then went to Naval Base School, staying at a relative's house. ⅰer graduating from Victoria School, he entered University of Singapore ⅰical College and graduated in 1973.

After his internship in a governmental medical institution, he worked as ⅰoctor in Block 157, Ang Mo Kio Avenue 4 since 1976. Dr. Kok allowed to interview him in his clinic although I did not have an appointment ⅰh him and a few patients were waiting. He discussed about his experience ⅰtudying in Hakka and humbly said that he was just an ordinary person, ⅰving patients wholeheartedly. Because a doctor in Singapore usually works entire day and on Saturdays too with few days off, Dr. Kok could not ⅰntain contact with the Tekong Island residents. He heard that some ⅰmer residents lead good lives in Singapore and serve the association well.

ⅰbert Lim Liang Chai (林两才)

ⅰrn in 1955, Albert Lim Liang Chai lived on Pulau Tekong Kechil. When ⅰdying in the elementary school, Lim had to take a boat to Pulau Tekong attending English classes. After 1967, like other children of the right ⅰ, he had spent half an hour taking a ferryboat to Changi Village in the ⅰly morning and transferred to Bus No. 2 for Changkat Changi Secondary ⅰool 4 km away until Secondary Four. After completing national service,

Lim started to navigate the Tug Boat in Pasir Panjang. He had also be a boatman in Clifford Pier in 1978. With these working experiences a understanding about the industries, Lim stepped into the business of mari gasoline. In 1985, Lim cooperated with one of his friends and bought a sma scale passenger boat in Tanjong Rhu.

Lim knew well about the trend of the market and targeted his custom on Crew Boat of Oil Rig in Jurong West. Now, his corporation, Cast Laun Service Pte Ltd., owns 30 boats, with over 100 employees. The market h been expanded to Outside Port Limit.

In the interview with Lim in his office in Golden Mile Complex, L: said that the reason for his success was that he fitted in with the communi in Jurong East where he was resettled by the government when he le Tekong Island in 1983. He also worked in the Nan Yang Citizens Consultati Committee. Now Lim is the Grass Roots Leader of Hong Kah GRC. As had been educated in English, he reads Straits Times. As a Chaozhoue: Malay is his second language. Lim's wife, a Hakka descendant and a form Tekong resident, is also his Chinese teacher. With the achievement in h career, Lim moved to his house in Upper Thomson. Now he has thr daughters and a son and regards himself as a common Singaporean. Li was conferred the Public Service Medal in 2010.

Lee Tong Soon (吕同顺)

Lee Tong Soon was born on Tekong Island in 1958. His father came sou from China at the age of 16 years. Lee had been very independent since h childhood because there were many children in his family (seven boys and fi girls) so his parents were involved with work. As for Lee's education, aft graduating from Pulau Tekong Primary School, he entered the Changk; Changi Secondary School in Singapore. Later, he finished high-school cours at Chung Cheng High School and went to Nanyang University. At th time, English was the principal language used in the university rather tha Chinese, which put him under a lot of pressure as he had been educated i Chinese in the past 12 years. Lee's determination helped him survive in th three-year university life and graduated in 1983. By then the university ha been transformed into National University of Singapore.

When Lee worked as an estate executive in HDB (Housing & Develop ment Board), he found himself unable to break through or be promote further in a governmental system where English was used as the mai language of communication. He was determined to give up this job, whic was usually considered to be secure and for life, and decided to be property agent. With 8 years of experience in HDB, he was recruited b onalds as it decided to establish a branch store in HDB Town, Lee hired as an industry manager since his expertise helped in expanding for branch stores. Lee was not satisfied with his life though he worked multinational company with a monthly salary of S$5,000. He never up the idea of establishing his own business. When his older brother Tong Guan (吕同观) came to Singapore from Thailand and learned ook shark's fin from Chaozhouese in 1991, Lee Tong Soon took his her's advice to start their own business. Due to insufficient capital, they ted three other friends to be shareholders. Each one of the shareholder ided S$50,000 to establish their first restaurant, Thai Village Seafood aurant, on East Coast Road. The restaurant occupied only 1,800 square and accommodated less than 80 customers at a time. Most of the affairs managed mainly by Lee brothers. Lee Tong Soon was in charge of inistration and management and his brother was responsible for the hen. Lee Tong Soon had no experience in restaurant management, so ad to learn from scratch. The initial days of starting a restaurant were gh because there was only a staff of 15, including the Lee brothers, who t deal with everything like cleaning and preparation. Lee Tong Soon trained during the period and learned a lot about the management of a aurant.

With the cooperation of Lee brothers on internal and external affairs, the aurant went profitable after a year of commencing its operations. The net fit was up to S$20,000 to S$30,000 in the second year. Accordingly, Lee g Soon prepared to expand the site of the restaurant after his first one steady. The first branch was closed three months after it was inaugurated to many factors, yet Lee was not frustrated. In 1994, he started over in and opened another branch in Oasis, in which the turnover on the t day was up to S$10,000. The business soon started flourishing and it has n the branch with the highest profit. (This branch was moved to Leisure ll because Oasis was transformed as a Sports Hub in 2009.) In 1996, the rd and the fourth branches were opened in Jurong and Seaview Hotel, pectively; the fifth branch was inaugurated in Admiralty Country Club in 7, and this one was the largest branch among all Thai Village restaurants, upying 6,500 square feet and accommodating more than 400 people. That iod could be regarded as the climax of Thai Village in Singapore.

During 1991 to 1997, there were five branches of Thai Village in gapore. Since the business had been profitable in Singapore, the restau- t was expanded to Indonesia. Lee Tong Soon said that the idea was posed by an Indonesian frequenter who planned to invest 80% of the ital and to share half of the profit. Lee did not have any reason to

turn down such a good opportunity, so the first branch in Indonesia was
Surabaya, which was the first step of expanding the business in Indones
During 1997–1998, the global financial meltdown had a great impact
Southeast Asia. Even though the business in Singapore and Indonesia w
struggling to survive, the economy in China was booming, which seemed
be a good investment destination. At that time, Lee and other shareholde
chose Shanghai as the first location, which Lee Tong Soon considered as
coincidence. The board chairman of Man Po Boutigue Hotel (新华路万宝酒)
invited Thai Village to set up a branch in the hotel and all the equipme
would be provided. Lee seized the opportunity and cautiously prepared f
the investment. He suggested that all the shareholders should offer capi
without drawing on the fund of Thai Village. In this way, the investme
risk would be lowered to the minimum so that the parent company wou
not be affected if the investment failed.

The first branch of Thai Village in Shanghai was not large, occupyi
only 1,000 square meters with 12 separate dining rooms. At the firs
the revenue was not as good as expected for the turnover in the fir
three months was only 300,000 RMB (around S$60,000). The public prai
had not spread around until six months later and the turnover increase
stably. Then the monthly turnover was up to one million RMB (arou
S$200,000), so customers even had to make a reservation two days earlie
The shareholders of Thai Village were encouraged by the success of th
first branch in China, and they planned to open the second branch
Sunshine Hotel on Hongqiao Road (虹桥路). This branch was three tim
larger than the first one (3,000 square meters with 30 dining rooms) and i
business soon went stable because of the reputation of the first branch. Th
monthly turnover even reached five million RMB (around S$ one million
Based on the success of Thai Village in Shanghai, hotels in other cities als
invited Thai Village to set up branch in the hotel. These hotels had encin
offers, asking for no extra capital but only human resources of managemer
from Thai Village. The branches in Shanghai, Qingdao (青岛) and othe
cities were managed with this plan and it laid the groundwork of Tha
Village in China. In 2000, another method of management was adoptec
The name "Thai Village" was used by franchise stores, which adopted th
food ingredients, such as shark's fin or abalone, and cooking methods of Tha
Village. By applying such management methods, Thai Village was able t
earn management fees.

On 28 April 2000, Thai Village had its IPO in Singapore in orde
to promote its brand. Registering the brand in China also brought th
restaurant preference and convenience in the investment. The business c

i Village grew stably and the revenue from China became the main source
ie restaurant's profits.

Lee Tong Soon attributed Thai Village's steady success in Singapore
China to his Chinese educational background. Numerous students from
iese school tended to establish business by their own for the purpose
chieving something because they could hardly have a place of their
in the so-called "mainstream society" in Singapore. It was essential
inderstand the culture and history of China if one plans to create his
rprise in China. When one is taught the language without the culture
history behind, he is like a body without soul and is not capable of
ctive communication with others.

Lee Tong Soon never ignored his family because of his work. He
impanies his wife and children on weekend outings whenever he is in
iapore. In addition to his business and family, he also cherishes old
idships. When he is in Singapore, he would visit his old friends, chatting
. coffee shop. He does not pursue the way of life of the upper class nor
s he engage in social activities. On 22 July 2007, Thai Village allowed
o have a gathering in one of its branch in Changi Village so that old
dents of Tekong Island could enjoy the buffet and help us conduct this
arch.

Ng Yin Kwee (吴应贵博士)

Ng Yin Kwee was born in 1961 in a rather poor family with 8 siblings.
family was located at Kampong Pasir beside the beach. Ng's father ran
mall grocery store, purchasing local products to resell the products to
ilesalers at Kampong Selabin. Similar to other villagers, Dr. Ng attended
au Tekong Primary School's Chinese section. He studied further and
ipleted his secondary education at Changkat Changi secondary school.

Dr. Ng graduated from Singapore Polytechnic and worked as a Marine
gineer in Exxon Tanker Fleet in the period from 1983 to 1985. He pro-
ded to obtain a B.Eng. from the University of Newcastle upon Tyne
1988. He pursued his Ph.D. at Queen's College and Whittle Research
ioratory in Cambridge University with Commonwealth Scholarship. He
ained a PG Diploma in Teaching Higher Education. NIE-NTU in 1955.

Dr. Ng is an Associate Professor and Assistant Chair (Alumni) at the
iool of Mechanical and Aerospace Engineering at Nanyang Technological
iversity.

Besides publishing papers in international journals, he also attends
ernational conference proceedings. He has co-edited five books and co-
thored a book "*Compressor Instability with Integral methods*" published

by Springer (2007). Dr. Ng also served as a committee member of Gr₂
Root organization.

Lye Soo Choon (赖素春)

Lye Soon Choon was born in 1971 on Tekong Island and went to P₂
Kindergarten. Later she moved to Singapore with his family and studi
in Bedok View Primary School. After that, he went to Anglican High Schc
and then graduated from Nanyang Junior College.

After graduating from National University of Singapore Arts & Soc
Science Faculty, Lye worked as an executive secretary in Char Yo.
(Dabu) Association. In 2003, she worked as Research officer, Oral Histo
Department, and has worked as a researcher. Nowadays, he takes advanta
of the time after work, studying for a degree of Ph.D. at Amoy Universit₃

Although Lye had migrated to Singapore, when she studied in prima
school, she had lived across from Da Jing Tou (大井头) in Kampong Selabi
Her great grandmother purchased eggs from villagers and sold them in t₃
market in Changi Village every day, so Lye's memory of her childhood w
very clear. She helped us a lot in the selection of the files from oral histo
archives and saved us valuable time in conducting this research.

5.4. Conclusion

An official of the Singapore Land Authorities, Lim Chin Joo, was aware of tł
residents' helplessness and sadness while he was dealing with the migratio.
As a witness to the history, he said,

> In the process of eliminating the old for new, some people's feelings might
> have been hurt and individual interests sacrificed. It happens in every country
> and every society. Even after many years, the residents from Tekong Island
> get together sometimes and organized an association. How much they miss the
> time they lived on Tekong Island! If they had a choice, they would definitely
> choose to stay there. Inspite of poverty, they regarded the life on the island
> as easy and carefree. If they continued to reside on the island, the schedule of
> national development would have been delayed. There are various alternatives
> for social reform or national progress. No matter which choice is decided, the
> price had to be paid. Is the sacrifice of worth? If the same event happened in
> a different environment and was dealt in a different way, the outcome would be
> different. I hope that those people's sacrifices are not be ignored while everybody
> is celebrating Singapore's achievement. We are supposed to heal the wounds that
> every period had left. While we feel proud of what we have achieved, don't forget
> the predecessors' sacrifice.[21]

---

[21] *Lianhe Zaobao* (Singapore), 9 September 2007.

The above text is worth thinking about. Singapore owns its achievements developments to the efforts and sacrifices of many people. Although ong Island's residents were just ordinary people, they quietly dedicated t they had to their country. The simple society on Tekong Island red a harmonious atmosphere between different ethnic groups. Their e relationship and affection seemed to fit in with nature. However, this of relationship gradually disappeared with development. The bond veen people and their land was sacrificed for the development of the itry. The residents of Tekong Island, who paid the inevitable price for country's progress, had no choice but to bury their memories of the id deep in their hearts.

CHAPTER 6

Conclusion

society on Tekong Island mainly comprised people of Chinese and
ay origin, with Indians numbering around ten. The combination of races
Tekong Island was similar to that in Singapore since both societies
e composed of migrants. Human migration has occurred since ancient
es and is a part of social progress. However, until recently, theory and
vant research on migration had not been developed. At present, there
abundant theories and research in this field, such as the push and pull
ory. In this theory, it is maintained that human migration is influenced
the society of the original residency in the situation of free economy
migration. People opt to migrate to a new place, searching for a better
ig environment, because of the desire to improve their lives. That is,
social or economic factor that attracts people to migrate to another
e is the pull force; on the contrary, the unfavorable condition of the
inal residency is the push force. It is evident that not only the push
e of the original residency but also the pull force of the target residency
cts human migration. During the rule of Ming and Qing dynasties, large
abers of people in the southeastern areas of China (particularly Fujian
Guangdong provinces) migrated overseas, and Tekong Island was one
heir options. The push force resulted from insufficient land, increasing
ulation and poverty and the pull force of the target residency, such as
theast Asia, might have been the abundance of land, sparse population
more opportunities of employment. The history of human migration
olves the interaction of many factors, and the migration on Tekong Island
ne part of history.
Relevant research has focused on the adaptation and assimilation of
grants rather than the reason, motivation or the pattern of migration, no
tter the conventional perspective of pull and push force or globalization.
e studies no longer focus only on a single localized community; instead,
field has been expanded in order to explore the cultural differences and
areness among migrants. A recent example is that of the Overseas Chinese
nmunity, which earlier used to be involved in the expansion of Chinese
iety but has now shifted its emphasis to subjectivity and uniqueness.

Identification of the target residency and potential cultural conflict are n
topics in this field.[1]

Although the focus of research has been on migrants' assimilation
resistance in the settlement, it has now shifted to the concept of diaspo
The Overseas Chinese are no longer an isolated group who have barricad
themselves from the mainstream society. Compared to previous researc
which places emphasis on the adaptation and development of an individu
migrant, most Overseas Chinese are concerned about and maintain conta
with their motherland and diaspora communities.[2] In addition to the p
and push force, the Overseas Chinese society was formed based on migran
network, as was the society of Hakka and Chaozhouese. Accordingly, t
main groups were formed on Tekong Island. The first- or second-generati
migrants on Tekong Island identified themselves as Chinese, and the
target was to return to their homeland in glory. These migrants we
concerned about Chinese affairs, as is proven by their support in the an
Japanese war.

When migrants move to a new land, they face both economic and soci
problems. Alfred Sauvy argued that the process of migration is not comple
until the migrant has experienced three phases: settlement, adaptation ar
total assimilation.[3] When there is a larger divergence in the cultures betwee
the homeland and target residency, migrants may take more time in settlir
down and may find it difficult to adapt to the new environment. By contras
the smaller the difference in cultures between the two regions, the easier
can be for migrants to proceed with their new lives. This theory can I
proved by the example of Hakka from Indonesia, who are of Chinese origi
Although the presence of both Chinese and Malays on Tekong Island w;
unusual, these two groups were able to accept and influence each other
cultures and work together despite their cultural differences.

Before the migration of the Chinese, their homesickness and the
close relationship with Tekong Island are discussed, the migration of othe

---

[1]By studying re-immigration, displacement and diaspora, one can have a better idea about th
thoughts of the Chinese in the lower strata of the society to discover the lost history which is n
overshadowed by China's history.

[2]Zhai, ZX (翟振孝) (2006). *Migration, Cultures and Identities: The Social Construction ar
Transnational Networks of Burmese-Chinese Immigrant Communities in Yangon, Jhonghe, ar
Toronto.* Unpublished dissertation, National Tsing Hua University, Institute of Anthropology.

[3]Yang, CR (杨聪荣) and Lan, QS (蓝清水), From Returned Overseas Chinese to Foreig
People — The History of Taiwanese in Indonesia and the Influence of Hakka Cultu
(《从归侨到外籍–印度尼西亚台湾人移民的历史过程,兼谈客家文化的影响》), see *The 3rd Crossing Bo
der and Wander* — International Conference held by Graduate School for Social Tran
formation Studies of Shih Hsin University (《世新大学社会发展研究所主办第三届 "跨界流离
国际学术研讨会(2006)》), p. 9.

ese-origin people to Tekong Island will be explored. After World War
he Chinese in Indonesia opted to migrate to other countries due to
-Chinese riots in the 1960s. Their migration was indeed affected by
tical and social problems irrespective of whether the migrants who
wed the "Chinese culture" moved to China, Taiwan or other countries.
ae discussion of the anti-Chinese riot in Indonesia, the Taiwanese scholar
g Cong Rong (杨聪荣) argued that persistent riots are supposed to be
stigated from both political and social perspectives, such as the shift
egime in Indonesia at that time. Therefore, Chinese issues cannot be
ussed alone.[4] Because of the unstable political and social environment in
onesia, the Chinese in Indonesia chose to migrate to other regions. Even
r the riots, the Overseas Chinese did not return to Indonesia and stayed
seas.

> In retrospect of the history of Indonesia, there are some similarities in the four
> riots. In the first place, every riot took place when there was a power transfer in
> Indonesia. ... Every time power transfer happened, wars or bleeding events were
> triggered as well. It was the time when those events resulted in anti-Chinese riots.
> It can be said that Chinese would be sacrificed when the regime was altered.[5]

Chinese who suffered in the riots left Indonesia and migrated to China
Taiwan in the 1960s. Around 200 of the Chinese arrived at Changzhi
wnship in Pingdong County and some Chinese resided near Longtan
wnship in Taoyuan County. The factors that affected the migration
Hakka from Indonesia now changed from the anti-Chinese events to
asnational marriage. Four main reasons can be identified for the migration
he Hakka from Indonesia to Taiwan: to pursue further studies, as a result
anti-Chinese riots and as a result of marriage or matchmaking.[6]
In the 1960s, most of the Chinese who moved from Indonesia to Taiwan
e Hakka and the majority resided close to each other. In addition to the
guage, the culture of the Hakka from Indonesia is almost similar to that
Taiwan. The Hakka then established their own community network with
p from their relatives or friends.

---

ng, CR. *The History of the Riot, Ethnic Relationship and Political Shift: The Power
nsfer and Anti-Chinese Riot in the History of Indonesia* (《暴动歷史 · 族群关系与政治变迁 :
尼西亚歷史上的政权转移与反华暴动》). See *Annual Conference of Studies Project on South-
: Asia* (1999) held by Academia Sinica (《中央研究院东南亚区域研究计划主办台湾的东南亚区
央研究院东南亚区域研究计划主办台湾的东南亚区 域研究年度研讨会》), p. 24.
ng, CR. *The History of the Riot, Ethnic Relationship and Political Shift: The Power Transfer
: Anti-Chinese Riot in the History of Indonesia*, p. 20.
ng, CR and Lan, QS, *From Returned Overseas Chinese to Foreign People — the History of
wanese in Indonesia and the Influence of Hakka Culture*, p. 12.

The experience of the Chinese in Myanmar was quite similar to th of those in Indonesia. Because of the activities of the national police Myanmar and hostile attitude toward Chinese, as well as the anti-Chine riots in Rangoon in 1967, the Chinese in Myanmar lived in fear.

> In 1960s, many Chinese in Myanmar felt disappointed as the military government restrained the economy and culture among Chinese. Therefore, they planned to move to other countries and some of them arrived at Taiwan. In the late 1960s and early 1970s, the Canadian government loosened the restriction of immigration so some of the Chinese in Myanmar chose to migrate to Canada. Some Chinese also first moved to Taiwan, Hong Kong or Macau and then migrated again to Canada, regrouping in Toronto.[7]

The autocratic government and unstable society in Myanmar prompt the migration of Chinese. Compared to Myanmar, the economy in Taiw had developed rapidly after the 1980s and its people gradually emerged fro poverty after World War II. As the Chinese in Myanmar were not fair treated and there were not many job opportunities, they decided to migra overseas. The first choice for the Chinese in Myanmar would be Taiwa Hong Kong or Macau because they may not be rich enough to move American or European countries and were attracted by the prevalence Chinese culture in those areas. Chinese who arrived at Taiwan in the 196 scattered and resided in Tao-yuan, Zhong-li or Nan-tou. After the 196C some of the Chinese from Myanmar gathered at Hua-Xin Street in Zhon ho, calling themselves *myanmapyipyan* (Chinese from Myanmar). As the way of life was different from that in Taiwan, the Taiwanese used to call th place they lived as "Myanmar Street."[8] Indeed, the Chinese from Myanm were different from the local people in Taiwan in food, attire, religion an the awareness of ethnic identification. Their experience of migration an memory can be verified by the Chinese from Indonesia at that time.

After Chinese Civil War ceased in 1949, the Kuomintang retreated t Taiwan and only part of its troops was left in Yunnan to continue fightin During the period from 1950 to 1953, the troops had adopted guerril warfare in the border of Thailand and Myanmar. With the assistance c UN, the first group of soldiers was sent to Taiwan. The last group of th soldiers was sent to Taiwan in 1961, so there were communities establishe by the family of the troops in northern, middle and southern Taiwan. In th

---

[7]Zhai, ZX (2006). *Migration, Cultures and Identities: The Social Construction and Transnation Networks of Burmese-Chinese Immigrant Communities in Yangon, Jhonghe, and Toronto*, p. 12? Unpublished dissertation, National Tsing Hua University, Institute of Anthropology.
[8]Zhai, ZX (1995), Experiences and identities: The ethnic formulation of immigrants in Chunghe Taiwan. Unpublished thesis, National Taiwan University, Dept of Anthropology.

s, two migrant communities were constructed in Jiyang Village, Meinong
nship[9]: Jingzhong Xin Village and Chenggong Xin Village. In Ligang
nship, Pingdong County, Xinguo Xin Village and Dingyuan Xin Village
also established. These villages were built by Kuomintang government
he soldiers and their family who retreated from the border of Yuannan
Myanmar in 1961.[10]

n early times, scholars who studied migrants maintained that the
rants may be gradually integrated into the society and regard themselves
embers of the local community. As the Chinese saying goes, "Another
e would be one's hometown if he stays there long enough." However,
eality, migrants do not cut off ties with their motherland. Many people
their hometowns and have constant interaction with it, thereby showing
r yearning for their homeland. The reason the Chinese from Myanmar
structed Thai temples was that they struggled to identify with the
ples in Taiwan. They felt more familiar with and experienced a sense of
nging with Burmese temples.[11] They even brought their relatives from
nmar to Taiwan and bought daily necessities from Myanmar; they con-
ed with their neighbors in Burmese, which showed how much they missed
r homeland. Their yearning could also be gleamed from their religion,
omy, politics and other social issues. Accordingly, it is not difficult to
erstand how strong their cohesive force and ethnic awareness was.

It can be comprehended that most of the Chinese who had migrated to Chungho or
Toronto returned to Myanmar for visiting their relatives, travel, religious sacrifices
repair, initiating Chinese education, assisting those children of Chinese study further in Taiwan and marrying in Myanmar after the Burmese government opened
itself to other countries in the 1990s. They invested their money, ran their business, donated funds to temples and purchased religious instrument and costumes
for cultural activities in Myanmar; they also bought and sold Burmese newspapers,
magazines, books, tapes, cassettes, disks, foods, medicines, cigarettes and other
daily supplies in order to keep continuous relationship with their hometown.[12]

Similar to the Chinese from Myanmar who missed their homeland, the
inese from Indonesia reproduced the style of construction of their houses

, SZ (谢世忠) (2004), *Tourism and Ethnic Transition: Progress of Returning Home of Non-
nese Military Dependents in Taiwan, Myanmar and Thailand (2/2)*. Taipei: National Science
ncil.

e, LS (2007) *Study of Ethnic Relationship and Cultural Interaction: Jiyang Li, Jidong Li and
Li in Meinong Town as Examples*, p. 6. Taipei: Council for Hakka Affairs, Executive Yuan.

hai ZX, *Migration, Cultures and Identities: The Social Construction and Transnational
works of Burmese-Chinese Immigrant Communities in Yangon, Jhonghe, and Toronto*, p. 83.
ublished dissertation, National Tsing Hua University, Institute of Anthropology.

hai ZX, *Migration, Cultures and Identities: The Social Construction and Transnational Networks
urmese-Chinese Immigrant Communities in Yangon, Jhonghe, and Toronto*, p. 158. Unpublished
ertation, National Tsing Hua University, Institute of Anthropology.

in Taiwan. Compared to conventional three-section compound or Hak
buildings, the "overseas house" looked unique among the traditional hou
in Taiwan. The Indonesian style of dressing was exquisite and delicate a
was different from the straw rain cape worn by the farmers in Hakka villag
The Chinese from Indonesia did not mean to show off or dress formally t
they had been used to wear that kind of clothes in Indonesia and continu
to maintain their style of dressing in Taiwan.

> The Chinese from Indonesia did not intentionally dress ostentatiously; they just
> followed their original Indonesian style of dressing. The clothes they had brought
> to Taiwan were very different what the farmers wore in Taiwan who worked hard
> and led a simple life.[13]

Residents of the villages that were established after World War II form
their own groups. They were excluded by the wattled "wall" from the outsi
world, which[14] made it difficult for them to join other groups. Such cohesi
force and awareness to resist the outside world existed in almost eve
military dependent's village. In a closed environment, people are able
bring back memories for the purpose of preserving and passing on the cultu
of their hometown. In his research studying Yuannan Village in Taoyua
Xie Shi Zhong pointed out that, in the past 50 years, the second-, even t
third-generation residents in the villages had been immersed in a society
multiple races and foreign culture.[15] These migrants, in fact, did not stay
a closed community all the time. Although they stepped into the Taiwane
society to experience a different culture, they still missed their hometown

> In a convention, people sang during prayers. The elderly were intoxicated in
> the atmosphere of the singing so that they could pass the time; the people in
> their middle age wished for success in their job; farmers sang for good harvest;
> businessmen sang for making a fortune in the market; young people or couples
> might dance with their friends; teenagers could sing to please each other. Though
> these people had different wishes, they were all immersed in the melody of
> the songs. Nowadays, singing is indispensable for those people from Yunnan to
> celebrate in family parties or national festivals.[16]

---

[13]Lee, LS (2007). *Study of the Internal Relationship and Cultural Interaction in Hakka: ChangZ
Town of Pingtong County as an Example* (《客家族群的内在关系与文化接触：以屏东县长治乡为例
Taipei: Council for Hakka Affairs, Executive Yuan.

[14]The wattled wall was not exclusively used by the migrants to delimit their villages. It w
acquired easily and is used in this research to symbolize a barrier differentiating the migrants an
other people.

[15]Xie, SZ (2003) *Recognition and Ethnic Awareness: Self-recognition of Non-Chinese in Yunna
Village, Taoyuan County (2/2)*. Taipei: National Science Council.

[16]Taoyuan County Government, *The Military Dependant's Village and Taiwan, Responsibili
and Glory — A Troop from Yunnan* (〈眷村与台湾。责任与光荣 – 来自云南的部队〉), see *Arts an
Culture in Taoyuan* (2007), p. 4.

.t can be observed from the above examples that the residents on Tekong
₁d once experienced poverty in their homeland. Due to the government's
₁ption, they had no choice but to migrate for other means of livelihood.
residents had a tough time adapting to the new environment, although
₁r experience was different from that of the Chinese from Indonesia and
₁nmar. They all missed their homeland and tried to continue living like
˙ did in the past. When in company of people from the same country,
˙ could joyfully revisit the experience of living in their homeland.
The reason migrants travelled huge distances to Southeast Asia was not
˙ for the search for a stable life but also to make themselves part of the
land. It was no easy task for them to survive when they first arrived at
₁ew place, so the first challenge was to adapt to the existing culture of the
land, while simultaneously preserving their own culture. However, the
₁rants' homesickness would not hinder them from taking control of their
₁. On the contrary, their ethnic features were manifest and they were
without goals. The way they proclaimed their religion and promoted
₁nese education enabled these migrants to maintain their culture. The
₁nese migrants gradually established their business on Tekong Island.
₁e migrants went into trade, some were interested in agriculture and
₁rs were engaged in fishing. The confirmation of a way of living stabilized
₁r lives. These migrants chose this land as their home and became the
₁ters of the island. Perhaps the new residence replaced the memory of
hometown and became the hometown of the following generations, but
y would continue to miss their motherland.
Ethnic harmony was one of the features of Tekong Island. Even though
₁re were great cultural differences between Chinese and Malays, not much
₁culty was caused during the process of ethnic fusion. Both communities
˙e able to embrace each other in harmony and gradually stepped into
path of integration. The ethnic gap was also reduced when the two
₁ups lived together on Tekong Island so there was no ethnic conflict as
Singapore. Within the Chinese, the Hakka and Chaozhouese peacefully
˙d together as their cultures were similar. On Tekong Island, there was no
₁flict or confrontation; instead, the ethnic relationship was peaceful and
₁monious.
The society of Tekong Island was composed of migrants. Since the
₁grants had lived on the island for one, even two generations, the "new
₁d" had become their hometown. The migrants recognized the island and
₁structed a close relationship with it. On Tekong Island, the residents had
₁erienced a lot of hardships together, including the anti-Japanese move-
₁nt, Japanese's occupation, British government's ruling, self-rule, accession

Street view of Kampong Selabin.

Street view of Kampong Selabin, now overgrown with trees and weeds.

to Malaysia and subsequent independence. All these events influenced th
residents to different degrees and the only thing that did not change wa
that they all lived on this island as usual. However, the independenc
of Singapore did affect their lives. With rapid urban development, th
residents in the country were attracted to living in cities. Due to rapi
urbanization and industrialization of Singapore, the residents who had bee
relying on agriculture as a mode of living faced difficulties. Soon Tekon
Island, a remote place with low economic value, became the first plac

British Army Exclusive Wharf at Ladang during the colonial period.

Wharf of Kampong Selabin.

be commandeered by the government. Because Tekong Island did not
·e high economic value, the government converted it into a military
ining center. As soon as Singapore was fully developed, the government
·ested resources in developing Tekong Island. Therefore, the residents on
· island had no choice but to leave. In 1987, the last household moved
· of the island and the civilian society on Tekong Island thus ceased to
·st. The land had fostered many outstanding people and these people

with great career achievements, such as Ho Kiau Seng, the chairman
Nanyang Khek Community Guild, Lee Tong Soon, the owner of Thai Villa
seafood restaurant, Dr. Wu Ying Gui (吴应贵), Associate Professor in t
Department of Engineering at Nanyang Technological University, Dr. Zha
Hong Xin (张宏兴) and many other tertiary graduates.[17] All these form
residents of Tekong Island contributed to the development of Singapo
With the passage of time and changes in the society, the people on the isla
overcame difficulties and closely connected themselves to the land. In ord
to move along with the trend of development, the islanders had to coopera
with the government and give up their land to enter city life. The policy m
have forced the Tekong Island residents to leave the island, but the affecti
for their hometown did not disappear but rather strengthened as time we
by. The life on Tekong Island would be the most beautiful memory to ma
of its former residents.

---

[17]Tekong Island residents who graduated from Nanyang University include Chen Xi Wen (陈喜文
Chen Ya Shan (陈亚山), Luo Wen Guang (罗文光), Shi Shu Wei (施淑薇), Luo You Gang (罗幼刚
Qiu Dun I (邱敦意), Lai Nan Shan (赖南山), Li Li Zhen (李丽珍), and those who graduated fro
universities in Singapore were Luo Xiao Gang (罗小刚) and Luo Ji Gang (罗继刚). Lye Soo Choc
graduated from National University of Singapore. This information was provided by Lai Nan Sha

Appendix

ɔendix 1: Song of Rubber Tapper and Song of Picking ▸al Shells

Song of Rubber Tapper and the *Song of Picking Shells* were created by ɪ Sit Har, who had lived in Tekong Island in the 1940s. The two Hakka ɡs reflected the lives of residents on the island. They were discovered Ɔhen Poh Sheng (陈波生) from the tape of oral interviews in the Oral ɔory Department, Singapore. The lyrics were turned into words with cooperation of Hakka predecessors: Liang Xhao Hui (梁肇辉), Gao Hua ɪng (高华昌), Li Li Chen (李丽珍) and Chang Zheng Xing (张振兴)). The songs are as follows:

ɪg of Rubber Tapper

Tapping rubber at five with light.
Having breakfast at eight.
It's ten after rubber has been tapped and collecting firewood on the way.
Collecting Latex.
It's dusk and cloudy.
Rain falls and wind comes, all hard work is in vain.
Rain ruin latex collection and having rice with water for breakfast.
Plucking wild vegetable as no income for rice.
Straping waist belt and waiting for tomorrow.
Planting banana instead of rubber.
Sweet potatoe, topioca with tapping vegetable pickles.
Everybody works hard together.
Money is saved to support the family.
Go to field after harvesting rubber.
Cultivate field with a hoe.
Sun shines, Wind blows and rain falls.
The hill is full of topioca and others.
Weeds are rooted out for growing rice and others.
Vegetables and topioca are all around the hill.
As the rain season is coming, nothing to be afraid as food has been stored.
Harvest rubber in the morning and read in the afternoon.
Be busy supporting the family.
Study hard to rise in the society.
Raise poultry and pig, plant vegetable and sweet potato.
Get up at daybreak and work till night.
Finally have a plentiful harvest.

All the family is pleased with enough food.
It's worthy being industrious and thrifty.
Everybody knows it.

Lyricist: Chin Sit H

Song of Picking Shells

Have a meal after collecting latex.
A-niu goes to school in the afternoon.
Big brother picks shells in Kampong Permatang,
I stay at home for housework.
Go to Permatang after working.
The beach is clean on the ebb.
Four friends compete for picking shells.
Friendship might be hurt in the competition.
Everyone goes to different direction.
It's better to pick individual's shells.
All people are happy without competition.
While picking up the shell,
People hear fish swimming.
Fish are found in bottom of the hole.
Catch the fish with a spear.
The sound continues under the stone.
The stone is lifted.
Fish and clam are found and caught.
Fish is caught but hands are bitten.
The basket is filled with fish.
Return home fully supplied.
As the tide wane, crabs swagger east and west.
Chen takes a trap, waiting for the crab to come in.
Shells are picked, crabs and catfish are caught,
together with other fish and clams.
All are in high glee.
The tide is rising quickly,
or more fish would be caught.
Fish is fresh and soft.
Take it home for grandmother.

Return home while tide flow
with basket full of crab, fish and prawn

Plentiful of seafood need not purchased
you can fry, steam etc.
Labour after work is worthy.
It help to be part of house expenses
Whole family enjoy the food
Still able to give away to neighbors.

Lyricist: Chin Sit Ha

Source: Ying Fo Fui Kun Bulletin, Issue No. 16 (2008).

ҙendix 2: A Brief History of Tian Kong Buddhist Temple

ı Kong Buddhist Temple was the only temple that was moved to
'apore from Tekong Island. The expense of the reconstruction in
apore was met by the solatium of the temples' removal and donations
ı the followers on Tekong Island and Singapore. A brief excerpt of the
ᴐry of Tian Kong Buddhist Temple is presented in this book so that the
ᴅers are able to understand the history and how the reconstruction was
ᴣted of the temple.

ırces of Tian Kong Buddhist Temple on Tekong Island

ᴣ story of Tian Kong Buddhist Temple is enthralling but bizarre. The
ᴏt of the temple, Dai Liu Niang, came to Tekong Island from the southern
ᴏn of China when she was 19 years. With two sons and a daughter, her
ᴣand, Chen, made a living by fishing, rubber tapping, planted vegetables
 fruit by their own, leading a simple and poor life.
 The miracle occurred when Dai was aged 50 years, when she suffered from
ᴣird illness and no doctors could cure her. One day, Goddess Guanyin was
ᴑrn in Dai's body and offered two prescriptions and three spells on papers.
 took the medicine and drank the spelled water, and soon she became
ᴣscious. Since then, she had followed the instructions from Guanyin as the
ᴏnd identity of the god of sun to redeem the people in this world.
 Tian Kong Buddhist Temple was initiated by Dai and Liu Lun Chun
伦春) and it was located in Kampong Pasir Merah in the 1960s. Located
ᴣhe east and facing the west, the temple was next to the pond in Dai's
ᴣber farm with a green mountain in the back and faced a pond in the
ᴣt. The nearby environment was filled with singing of birds, fragrance of
ᴠers, green hills and clean water; what a picturesque scenery it was! With
ᴣ's endeavors, many followers went to the temple for worship and it was
ᴣinguished in Southeast Asia for its efficaciousness.
 In the 1970s, Tekong Island was commandeered by the government for
ᴣitary purpose. Dai did not like to watch the temple started by her closed
ᴠn. On 19 February 1984, Dai founded a community center, gathering
ᴏwers for Tienchao Buddhist Temple, Xi Hua Temple, Tuan Kong Beo
ᴍple, Jiang Fu Temple and residents from Kampong Selabin. The first
ᴨmittee meeting was held for the reconstruction of the temple. They
ᴌowed related regulations in Registry of Societies and elected for 10
ᴨmittee members and their positions.
 The chairman was Chen Tian Shui (陈添水), the secretary Ho Kim Fong
ᴦ金煌) and financial committee member Wang Shou Qing (王首清). The

committee members included Dai Liu Niang (who passed away in 1986), W
Ming Jun (温敏君) (who passed away in 1990), Tang Wan Ping (汤挽平) (w
passed away in 1993), Lu Mao Ming (卢茂明) (who passed away in 198
Huang Shuang Wang (黄双旺), Zhang Liang Bao (张良报) and Chen Rui
(陈瑞发). Chen Tian Shui was assigned to register the Tian Kong Buddh
Temple as a legal association. On March 15 of that year, the temple w
approved legal by Registry of Societies in Registration No. 1046.

In the same year, a location on Bedok North Ave 4 was selected a
the temple officially began to be constructed on 17 April 1990. In 19
the Tian Kong Buddhist Temple was inaugurated at the new premises. T
committee members of the temple in the first year were Chen Tian Sh
the chairman, He, Jin Huang, the secretary, Wang Shou Qing, the financ
committee member and other committee members: Huang Shuang Wan
Zhang Liang Bao, Chen Rui Fa, Dai Liu Niang (who passed away in 198
Wen Ming Jun (who passed away in 1990), Lu Mao Ming (who passed aw
in 1985) and Tang Wan Ping (who passed away in 1993).

The solatium donated for the reconstruction from Tian Kong Buddh
Temple, Tienchao Buddhist Temple, Xi Hua Temple, Tuan Kong B
Temple, was S$37,954.28 and that from Jiang Fu Temple was S$9,192.62.

Appendix 3: A Brief History of the Tuan Kong Beo Temple

Tuan Kong Beo Temple was one of the associations on Tekong Island ar
also the only legal association after the residents migrated to Singapor
Appendix 3 provides a brief report on the temple's history.

Tuan Kong Beo Temple had been called "Tekong Island Chaozhc
Corporation," which was organized as a community organization by migran
from Chaozhou. In the 1930s, the leader of the Chaozhouese, Huang Ge Ba
(黄歌保), who was also the owner of Yeh-chang Store, came up with the ide
to establish the organization for the purpose of enhancing the relationshi
between Chaozhouese and respecting Tuan.

At that time, the shrine of Tuan was placed in the custody of th
master of the shrine and it was worshipped by the public only on th
birthday of Tuan. The shrine would return to the master's house afte
the ceremony. After Huang Ge Bao, Tekong Island Chaozhou Corporatio
had been managed by Shen Mu Cun (沈木存) until early the 1960s. The
Huang Ge Bao's first son Huang Liang Mei (黄两梅) (owner of Shun Chen
(顺成号) store) was in charge of the affairs of the association in successio
to Shen. During Huang Liang Mei's period, he proposed to construct
building for the association and was supported by the Chaozhouese living o
Tekong Island and near the mouth of Johor River. They jointly funded th

hase of a building at 50, Kampong Selabin, as a location for Tuan Kong Temple and Tuan's shrine. The incumbent chairman Heng Shou Qing 訂清) has been in the position since the 1960s. Migrants from Chaozhou 1 in unity and assisted each other for many years.

The Chinese living near the mouth of Johor River also worshipped Tuan. or its title, the Chaozhouese called it Tuan Kung while the Hakka called 1an Kungyeh. After leaving Tekong Island, the Chaozhouese adopted the of Tuan as the name of the association.

In the 1980s, as Tekong Island was commandeered by the Ministry of ional Defense, its residents were forced to move to Singapore. Based on close relationship and affection between Chaozhouese, they had held 1y discussions and, according to Heng Shou Qing and Huang Xi Di's 田弟) suggestion, deciding to continue to maintain Chaozhou Corporation ice a new life with the spirit of mutual assistance. Then the abbot of Tian 1g Buddhist Temple, Dai Liu Niang (戴六娘), advised members of Tuan 1g Beo Temple, as well as other three temples, that they purchase lands n Housing Development Board so that the residents from Tekong Island e able to worship their gods in Singapore. The indemnification from government was managed by Tian Kong Buddhist Temple as funds for onstruction. In 1986, shrines of the gods were carried from Tekong Island he temporary wooden house in No. 51, Bedok North Ave 4, Singapore. ? construction of new temple was finished in 1994 and the migration of 1n Kong Beo Temple was thus final completed.

After studying local laws for nine years, it was decided to register 10zhou Corporation as a legal association and to adopt a younger irman. As the "Tuan Kong Beo (Teochew) Temple" was used as the e of Chaozhou Corporation when contacting with the government, it was ermined to use "Tuan Kong Beo Temple" as the name of the association, ich was approved by Registry of Societies on 4 July 1994.

At present, there are more than 100 members in the association of Tuan ng Beo Temple, and they have a reunion every year on lunar 15 December celebrate Tuan Pokung's birthday. The attendants include Hakka, former kong Island residents from Chaozhou and Chiung (琼) and those in the rison on Tekong Island. The opera in the celebration of Tuan's birthday uld last for two days so that people involved can recall the joyful time of ir the past and show their gratitude to gods.

Furthermore, whenever there is a funeral in any member's home, other mbers in the association would be informed to express their sympathy and er help. The spirit of the association is thus realized. As the consultant of : association, Huang Xi Di, said, "the friendship between residents from kong Island must continue because it's difficult to find it in urbanized

Singapore..." It is indeed valuable as Tuan Kong Beo Temple plays important role in encouraging its members to assist each other so that th continue to maintain friendship and affection for each other.

First Management Committe of Tuan Kong Beo (Teochew) Temple (Form in 1994) :

Chairman : Heng Siew Cheng(王首清)
Vice Chairman : Goh Gim Joo(吴锦裕)
Gen.Secretary : Lea Guan Chong(吕玩俊)
Asst.Secretary : Ng Boon Siang(黄文祥)
Treasurer : Tieu Ah Tee(张锡潮)
Assit. Treasurer : Ng Gek Keng(黄玉勤)
Recorder : Chinses : Goh Tang Song(吴丹松)
          English : Toh Chai Teck(杜财德)
Member : Ng Yang Khoon(黄炎坤)
         Ng Ee Son(黄天城)
         Heng Hup Koon(王学群)
Advisor : Ng Soi Tee(黄细弟)

Tuan Kong Beo (Teochew) Temple donated $3,500.00 for the publication this book.

Source: Tuan Kong Beo Temple.

Appendix 4: Distribution of Stores in Kampong Selabin

No		Note	No		Note
1	Le Quan Mei Tea House		26	Yi Chin Dental Clinic	
2	Nan Long Store	Retail of gas	27	Tong Chun Tang Chinese Medical Hall	
3	Gao Xing Imported Goods		28	Ho Xing Grocery Store	
4	Chuan Xing Grocery Store		29	Yu Tai Grocery Store	
5	Xin Ho Scooter Repair		30	Ho Tai Grocery Store	
6	Mei Ho Imported Goods		31	Yong Miao Sheng Chinese Medical Hall	
7	Mei Ho Imported Goods		32	Tian Cheng Grocery Store	With a factory of dried coconut
8	Chang Sheng Store	Seafood	33	Household	
9	San Li Tea House		34	Shun Cheng Store	Grocery, fruit and vegetables
10	Lian Xing Imported Goods & Bikes		35	Yuan Ho Silver Store	
11	Jia Li Eatery		35A	Household	Former Eng Wah School

(*Continue*

(*Continued*)

	Note	No		Note
Yong Xing Grocery Store		35B	Household	
Lien Shen Grocery Store		35C	Household	
Wan Ho Grocery Store		36	Household	
Household		37	Household	Former Oi Wah School and teacher's dorm
Guangdong & Fujian Association	Pork Seller on Level One	38	Silom Grocery Store	The only one grocery store owned by Malay
Xin Chang Grocery Store		39	Nan Fa Store	Food and beverage
Xin Chang Grocery Store		40	Tekong Seafood Satay	
Xie Da Bang Grocery Store		41	Household	In back of a bike store
You Cheng (Xiao Jin Fa Gold Store)		42	Household	Former tailor shop and Indian teahouse
Wan Xing Imported Goods		43	Household	
Jin Xing Imported Goods		44	Household	
Lien Xing Grocery Store		45	Xin Xing Grocery Store	
Yi Li Barber Shop		46	Xiu Bo Baber Shop	Former Oi Wah School
Xie Sheng Grocery Store		47	Household	It was once a factory processing dried coconuts
Household		67	Tuan Kong Beo Temple	
Household	Former tailor shop	68	Yeh-chang Store	A factory processing dried coconuts (once a pawnshop)
Household		69	Godown	Hsieh-ta-pang Godown
Household		70	Hai Li Teahouse	
Household	Majhong House, once a clinic before 1956	71	Tekong Seafood Restaurant	Former Hsin-chang Grocery Store and a godown
Household	Former bakery	72	Factory of dried coconut	Owned by Yeh-chang Store
Household		73	Household	
Household		74	Household	
Dental clinic	Former furniture store	75	Household	
Community center	Former Oi Wah School	75A	Household	

(*Continued*)

(Continued)

No		Note	No		Note
58	Household	Former Kelong, the dorm of workers	56A	Household	
59	Household		56B	Household	
60	Public toilet		56C	Household	Former Indian teahouse and a godown
61	Household		50A	Godown	Former Fish ball Noodles Store, Indian teahouse and the godown
62	Household	Former eatery	MR	The house of some Malay	
63	Household	Former laundry	S	Public bathroom	
64	Household	Former barber shop	D	Well	
65	Household	Former barber shop	T	Toilet	
66	Household	Dried bean curd factory			

Source: Loo Geuang Choon.

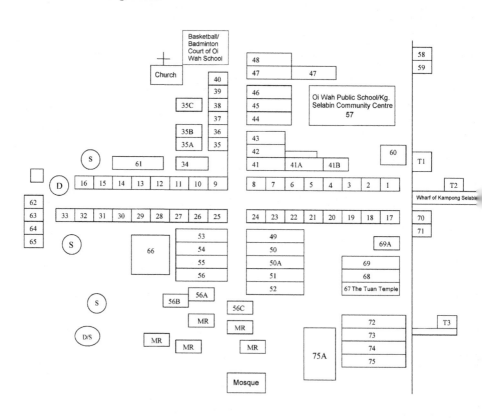

References

hinese References

odicals

yang Association (ed.) (1958). *Singapore Memorial Journal for 100 Year of Chiayang Association*. Singapore: Chiayang Association.

, *Association Journal*. (2006) Singapore: Singapore Federation of Chinese Clan Associations.

ing Committee of Federation of Clan Association (2005). *20 Years of Federation of Clan Association*. Singapore: Singapore Federation of Chinese Clan Associations.

YH (羅永享) (1986). *Special Issue of Periodical of Singapore Chinese Chamber of Commerce & Industry's 80th Anniversary*. Singapore: Chinese Chamber of Commerce & Industry.

ng YH (黃溢华) (ed.) (1985). *Special Issue of Periodical of Ee Hoe* Hean (怡和軒) *Club's 30th Anniversary 1895–1985*. Singapore: Ta-shui-niu Publishing.

utes of 26th Chinese Chamber of Commerce & Industry's 11th Board Conference (1953). Singapore: Chinese Chamber of Commerce & Industry.

etariat of Rubber Trade Association of Singapore (ed.) (1957). *1957 Yearbook of Rubber Trade Association of Singapore*. Singapore: Rubber Trade Association.

apore Tekong Island Chaochou Tuan Kong Beo Temple. (1985). Singapore: Tuan Kong Beo Temple.

Third Committee Conference of 10th Anniversary of Fujian Association. (1953). Singapore: Fujian Association.

l History Interviews — Tekong Island Oral History Project:

l History Interview with Abdullah bin Hassan, 2007.
l History Interview with Chen Chun Rong (陈春蓉), 2007.
l History Interview with Chen Xi Chou (陈细洲), 2007.
l History Interview with Guo Chun Lian (郭春莲), 2007.
l History Interview with Hong-Xia Guo (郭红霞), 2007.
l History Interview with Ho Lian Ying (何莲英), 2007.
l History Interview with Ho Mei Mei (何美妹), 2007.
l History Interview with Ho Wen Hui (何文慧), 2007.
l History Interview with Ho Yue Xi (何月惜), 2007.
l History Interview with Hong Chu Lan (洪竹兰), 2007.
l History Interview with Huang Bing Song (黄炳松), 2007.
l History Interview with Huang Chun Ying (黄春瑛), 2007.
l History Interview with Huang Ming Xuan (黄明轩), 2007.
l History Interview with Huang Sheng Jie (黄盛杰), 2007
l History Interview with Huang Xiang Gui (黄祥桂), 2007.
l History Interview with Lai Wan Qing (赖万清), 2007.
l History Interview with Antong Lee (李安东), 2007.
l History Interview with Li Li Zhen (李丽珍), 2007.
l History Interview with Li Zhu Zhen (李祝珍), 2007.
l History Interview with Lee Tong Soon (吕同顺), 2007.

Oral History Interview with Loo Geuang Fiyau (吕玩标), 2007.
Oral History Interview with Lea Guan Chong (吕玩俊), 2007.
Oral History Interview with Heng Siew Leng (王首龙), 2007.
Oral History Interview with Wang Shou Qing (王首清), 2007.
Oral History Interview with Huang Wen De (黄文德), 2007.
Oral History Interview with Yang Teng Gao (杨腾高), 2007.
Oral History Interview with Jaffar bin Kassim (耶亚华), 2008.
Oral History Interview with Zhang Cai Ying (张彩英), 2007.
Oral History Interview with Zheng Xi Mei (郑细妹), 2007.

Newspapers:

Lianhe Zaobao (Singapore), 1986, 1994, 2005, 2007.
Nanyang Siang Pau (Singapore), 1949–1964, 1982.
Sin Chew Jit Poh (Singapore), 1950–1964.
Petir (Singapore), 1972.

Publications:

An, HR (安焕然) and Jing, LL (劉莉晶) (eds.) (2007). *Migration and Exploitation of Hak* *from Johor.* Southern College Johooe Bahru, Persatuan Thoong Nyien (Hakka) Joh Bahoy.

Cai, MK (蔡明坤) and Wang, SH (王淑慧) (2005). *The Pokung Temple in Hakka Villa* *in Liudui and Neipu.* Taipei: Council for Hakka Affairs, Executive Yuan & SM Publishing Inc.

Chiang, HD (1978). A History of Straits Settlements Foreign Trade 1870–1915. pp. 8– Singapore: National Museum.

Chong, H (崇汉) (1992). *Loved Tekong.* Singapore: Changwu Publishing.

Chen, LF (陈烈甫) (1985). *The Singapore under Lee Kuan Yew's Ruling.* Taiwan: T. Commerce Press Ltd.

Chen, JX (陈厥祥) (1963). *The Chronology of Chimei.* Hong Kong: Chen, JX.

Chen, SB (陈少斌) (ed.) (2003). *Trace of Tan Kah Kee's deed — Brief Biography of famil* *of Chen Wenchueh & Chen Liushih in Chimei.* Xiamen: Chimei Overseas Chine Association, Chimei Study Society of Tan Kah Kee.

Chen, SS (陈世松) (ed.) (2005). *Theses of Migration & Hakka Culture Internation* *Conference.* Guilin: Guangxi Normal University Publishing.

Chen, WL (陈维龙) (1997). *Brief Introduction of Chinese Well-known Persons in Sout* *eastern Asian.* Singapore: The South Seas Society.

Choi, KK (崔贵强) (1990). *Recognition and Transformation of Singapore and Malays* Singapore: Singapore Nanyang Association.

Choi, KK (1994). *Chinese in Singapore — from A Trade Harbor to An Independe* *Country.* Singapore: Singapore Federation of Chinese Clan Associations.

Guoping (国平) (1962). *Rubber Industry in Malaya.* Singapore: World Book Co., Ltd.

Ho, BD (何炳棣) (1966). *History of Huiguan.* Taipei: Student Book.

Ho, KF (何金煌) (1993). *History Pulau Tekong & Tian Kong Buddhist Temple.* Singapor He, Jin Huang.

Huang, ZL (黄枝连) (1971). *Introduction of Chinese Society in Singapore.* Singapore: Wan Culture Corp.

Jian, JR (简炯仁) (2004). *Study of Villages in Nan-tzu-keng.* Kaohsiung: Kaohsiung Cit Archives.

Lee, KY (李光耀) (1998). *A Chronology 1923–1965.* Singapore: World Book.

Lee, KY (1998). *A Chronology 1965–2000.* Singapore: World Book.

Lee, KC (李炯才) (1989). *Pursuit of One's Country.* Taipei: Yuan-Liou Publishing.

LS (利亮时) (2007). *Study of Ethnic Relationship and Cultural Interaction: Jiyang Li, Jidong Li and Jiho Li in Meinong Town as Examples.* Taipei: Council for Hakka Affairs, Executive Yuan.

LS (2007). *Study of the Internal Relationship and Cultural Interaction in Hakka: ChangZhi Town of Pingtong County as an Example.* Taipei: Council for Hakka Affairs, Executive Yuan.

'Y (李威宜) (1999). *Transition of Chinese in Singapore: from Perspectives of Language Group, Communitarianism and Ethnicity.* Taipei: Tangshan Books.

YM (李玉梅) (1998). *The Independence of Singapore.* Singapore: National Heritage Board.

, CH (廖正宏) (1985). *Migration.* Taipei: San Min Book Co., Ltd.

KZ (林开忠) (1999). *Chinese Culture in Construction: Ethnicity, Country and Movement of Chinese Education.* Kuala Lumpur: Center for Malaysian Chinese Studies.

H Y (刘还月) (1999). *Hakka in Taiwan and Their Religion.* Taipei: Changmin Culture Ltd. Corp.

·seas Chinese Association in Singapore and Malaysia (新马侨友会) (ed.) (1992). *Malayan Anti-Japanese Army.* Hong Kong: Jianzheng Publishing.

apore Lianhe Zaobao (联合早报) (ed.) (1993). *Lee Kuan Yew' Political Statements in 40 Years.* Singapore: Newspapers Holdings Chinese Papers Group.

;, LF (宋龙飞) (1982). *A Research of Folklore Art.* Taipei: Art Venue Publishing.

ker, P (2001). *The No-Nonsense Guide to International Migration.* pp. 21–24. UK: New International Publication Ltd.

, KK (1949). *Collection of Tan Kah Kee's Discourse.* Singapore: Tan Kah Kee.

, KK (1979). *The Memoirs of Overseas Chinese in Southeastern Asia.* HK: Caoyuan Publishing.

, KK (2008). Opera and Society: Chinese Opera as an example. Unpublished honors thesis National University of Singapore, Department of Chinese Studies.

1g, FC (王甫昌) (2003). *Ethnic Imagination in Contemporary Taiwan.* Taipei: Socio Publishing.

1g, GW (王赓武) (1988). *Transaction and Chinese in Southeastern Asia.* Translated by Yao Nan. Hong Kong: Zhong Hwa Book Co.

1g, GW (1985). *China and Overseas Chinese.* Taiwan: The Commerce Press Ltd.

1g, GZ (王国璋) (1997). *Ethnic Politics in Malaysia 1955–1995.* Taipei: Tangshan Publishing.

1g, XW (王省吾) (1978). *Chinese's Migration Agencies 1848–1888.* San Francisco: Chinese Information Center.

, H (吴华) (1997). *History of Chinese Clan Association in Singapore.* Singapore: The South Seas Society.

, YH (吴元华) (1999). *Practical Decision — A Study of PAP and Government's Policy on Chinese 1954–1965.* Singapore: Lianbang Publishing.

, SZ (谢世忠) (2003). *Recognition and Ethnic Awareness: Self-recognition of Non-Chinese in Yunnan Village, Taoyuan County (2/2).* Taipei: National Science Council.

, SZ (2004). *Tourism and Ethnic Transition: Progress of Returning Home of Non-Chinese Military Dependents in Taiwan, Myanmar and Thailand (2/2).* Taipei: National Science Council.

, ZR (谢宗荣) (2003). *Religious Culture in Taiwan.* Taizhong: Morning Star Ltd. Co.

1, CH (颜清湟) (1992). *History of Overseas Chinese.* Singapore: Singapore Society of Asian Studies.

1, W (殷伟) (2003). *Gods in Chinese Religion.* Kunming: Yunnan People Publishing.

Yong, CF (杨进发) (1999). *Tan Kah-Kee: The Making of an Overseas Chinese Lege* [Translated by Lee, FC (李发沉)]. p. 10. US: Bafang Corp. World Scientific.

You, PS (游保生) and Lin, CY (林崇椰) (1984). *The Development of Singapore in the F 20 Years.* Singapore: Nanyang, Sin Chew Lianhe Zaobao.

Yu, YS (余英时) (1987). *Ethics of Chinese Religion in Recent Period and the Spirit Trader.* Taipei: Linkingbooks.

Zeng, XC (曾喜城) (1999). *A Study on Hakka Culture in Taiwan.* Taipei: National Taiw Library.

Zhong, XJ (钟锡金) (1984). *An Investigation of Chinese Ethnic Awareness in Singap and Malaysia.* Alo Star: Chihtu Books.

Zhu, LW (朱立文) (ed.) (1993). *A Study of Tan Kah Kee's Patriotism.* Beijing: Toc China Publishing.

Thesis of Academic Degree:

Chen, JT (陈金土) (1970). Relationship between Chinese Businessman, Clan Associati and Education: A Case Study of Nanyang University's Construction by Fujien C Association. Unpublished honors thesis, Nanyang University, Dept of History.

Huang, YQ (黄月群) (1972). *Shift of Population Distribution in Singapore from 1957 1970.* Unpublished honors thesis, Nanyang University, Dept of Geography.

Meng, ZH (孟智慧) (2004). A Study of identity of diaspora from research on cro in Qincen Farm and Shitao Farm. Unpublished thesis, Institute of Anthropolo National Tsing Hua University.

Pan, ZY (潘朝阳) (2003). Structure and space of traditional cultural areas in Taiwan: Ma as an example of cultural meaning in history and geography. Unpublished dissertatic Institute of Geography in National Taiwan Normal University.

Shi, LW (施丽雯) (2004). The multiple meanings of "Home": A case study on the life cou of the first generation residents in Hongmian Village. Unpublished thesis, Tungh University, Dept of Sociology.

Wu, ZB (吴中博) (1971). Population and usage of land on Tekong Island. Unpublish honors thesis, Nanyang University.

Xie, MH (谢美华) (2001). A study of village development in Annan District, Tain City and residents' living space. Unpublished thesis, National Kaohsiung Norm University, Dept of Geography.

Zhai, ZX (翟振孝) (1995). Experiences and Identities: The ethnic formulation of imm grants in Chungho, Taiwan. Unpublished thesis, National Taiwan University, Dept Anthropology.

Zhai, ZX (2006). Migration, cultures and identities: The social construction and transn tional networks of Burmese-Chinese immigrant communities in Yangon, Jhongh and Toronto. Unpublished dissertation, National Tsing Hua University, Institute Anthropology.

Articles:

Chin, SH (2008). Song of Rubber Tappers, *Journal of Yingho Clan Hall,* **16**, p. 15.

Dou, WJ, (1996). The rise and decline of Nanyang University — Analysis of the prospe of reconstructing Nanyang University. *Overseas Chinese History Studies,* **1**, pp. 20–2

Han, YS and Li, YL (1988). Introduction of Malayan Communist during the war, Secr of Malayan Communist. pp. 22–25. Singapore: Shing Lee Publishers Pte Ltd.

Lee, LS (2001). The educational policy and Chinese's response at early stage of Malaysia independence. *Asian Culture,* **25**, pp. 159–162.

Ma, R (2006). New thoughts of understanding ethnic group: Avoiding politicization on th minorities. In *Ethnicity and Society,* TT Wu (ed.), p. 80. Taipei: Wu-Nan Book Inc

, LF (1982). God of rice, officials in the government, Earth God: Introduction of Meinong. *Hansheng*, **12**, pp. 78–81.

, LF (1989). Hakka's Pokung Temple. *Hansheng*, **23**, pp. 65–69.

, YL (2006). Beyond the discipline and transition of migration studies in human geography: A comparison between Taiwanese anglophonic studies. *Journal of Geographical Science*, **43**.

uan County Government (2007). The military dependant's village and Taiwan, responsibility and glory — A troop from Yunnan, *Arts and Culture in Taoyuan*.

g, GW (2002). Chinese overseas: The past in the future. In *New Research Directions on the Chinese Overseas*, H Liu and JL Huang (eds.), pp. 39–59. USA: Global Publishing.

, CY (1987). The transformation of Chinese society in Singapore. In *Studies on Chinese Societies in Southeast Asia*, LY Yuan (ed.), pp. 15–104. Taipei: Zhong Zheng Book.

SZ (1997). Nationalism: The construction, scope and transformation — 50 years of Yunnan, Myanmar and Taiwan of ROC Army of Division 93. *Bulletin of the Department of Anthropology*, **52**, pp. 43–68.

GL (2006). From interaction to integration — A Study on people in Hochou. In *Ethnicity and Society*, TT Wu (ed.), p. 295. Taipei: Wu-Nan Book Inc.

YQ (1952). Studies on Ta Pokung. *Journal of the South Sea Society*, pp. 19–24.

, CR and Lan, QS (2006). From returned overseas Chinese to foreign people — the history of Taiwanese in Indonesia and the influence of Hakka Culture, *The 3rd Crossing Border and Wander*, International Conference held by Graduate School for Social Transformation Studies of Shih Hsin University, p. 9.

g, CR (1999). The history of the riot, ethnic relationship and political shift: the power transfer and anti-Chinese riot in the history of Indonesia. *Annual Conference of Studies Project on Southeast Asia*, Academia Sinica, p. 24.

g, CF (2001). Tan Kah Kee: No regret to revive Chinese. In *Start of an Enterprise and Root Protection: History of Chinese in Malaysia*, Lim, SH (ed.), pp. 1–40. Taipei: Academia Sinica Southeast Asia Project.

ng, MG (1999). Chapter 8: Race and ethnicity, In *Sociology and Taiwan Society*, Wang, ZH and Chu, HY (eds.), pp. 239–279. Taipei: Juliu Publisher.

ng, LS (2001). Tan Cheng Lock: A scholar-like politician. In *Correction and Trend: History of Chinese Politicians in Malaysia*, HQ Liang (ed.), pp. 25–54. Taipei: Academia Sinica Southeast Asia Project.

ng, ZM (2004). Development of Da Pokung in Hakka Society in Southeastern Asia, *Huaqiao University Journal*, **1**, p. 65.

er References:

rmation provided by Chen Ting Zhon.

rmation provided by Ho Kim Fong.

rmation provided by Kok Kim Leoong.

rmation provided by Lai Nan Shan.

n Ting Zhon, Ho Kim Fong, Kok Kim Leoong and Lai Nan Shan were former residents on Tekong Island.

English References

vernment Publications and Reports

7 *census of population, Singapore: Preliminary release no. 1–17*. Singapore: Government Printer, 1960.

nsus of population 1970, Singapore. Singapore: Department of Statistics, 1971.

nsus of population 1980, Singapore. Singapore: Department of Statistics, 1981.

Proceedings of the Legislative Council of the Federation of Malaya 18 March 1953. Ku
Lumpur: Government Printer, 1954.
Chua SC, *Report on The Census of Population 1957.* Singapore: Government Printer, 19
The Laws of the Colony of Singapore Volume 5. Singapore: Government Printer, 1955.

Official Documents

Pulau Tekong Malay School file. Singapore: National Archives of Singapore, Ref:ME38
Pulau Tekong School file. Singapore: National Archives of Singapore, Ref:ME3877.
Tengku Ahmad's letter of appointment (1949). Singapore: Malaya Heritage Centre.

Oral History Interview

Oral History Interview with Abdullah bin Ahmad. Singapore: Oral History Departme
1984.
Oral History Interview with Abu Bakar bin Hj. Abdul Halim. Singapore: Oral Histc
Department, 1986.
Oral History Interview with Abu Samah bin Awang. Singapore: Oral History Departme
1987.
Oral History Interview with Chin Sit Har (陈锡霞). Singapore: Oral History Departme
1987.
Oral History Interview with George T James. Singapore: Oral History Department, 19
Oral History Interview with HD Yusop bin Kassim. Singapore: Oral History Departme
1984.
Oral History Interview with Heng Siew Hiok(王守旭). Singapore: Oral History Departme
1984.
Oral History Interview with Heng Siew Leng(王首龙). Singapore: Oral History Depa
ment, 1982.
Oral History Interview with Jemaat bin Awang. Singapore: Oral History Department, 19
Oral History Interview with Lai Kok Siong(赖国祥). Singapore: Oral History Departme
1989.
Oral History Interview with Leong Teng Chit(梁定哲). Singapore: Oral History Depa
ment, 1982.
Oral History Interview with Lim Soo Gan(林树彦). Singapore: Oral History Departmer
1982.
Oral History Interview with Ng Ah Tong(黄亚忠). Singapore: Oral History Departmer
1984.
Oral History Interview with Ng Boon Tiang(黄文典). Singapore: Oral History Departmer
1982.
Oral History Interview with Ng Kia Cheu(黄镜秋). Singapore: Oral History Departmer
1982.
Oral History Interview with Ng Swee Chiang(黄瑞章). Singapore: Oral History Depar
ment, 1982.
Oral History Interview with Sia Seng Lan(佘胜兰). Singapore: Oral History Departmer
2000.
Oral History Interview with Wong Kwong Sheng(黄光盛). Singapore: Oral Histor
Department, 1982.

Newspapers

The Straits Times (Singapore), 1950–1964, 1985.

‹S

‹t Lau (1998). *A Moment of Anguish: Singapore in Malaysia and the Politics of Disengagement.* Singapore: Times Academic Press.

ld C, Brackman (1966). *Southeast Asia Second Front: The Power Struggle in the Malay Archipelago.* Singapore: D.Moore Press.

ndjuntak, B (1985). *Federalisme Tanah Melayu 1945-1963.* Petaling Jaya: Penerbit Fajar Bakti.

ıg, LK (1985). *Social Change and the Chinese in Singapore.* Singapore: University Press.

ng, HD (1978). *A History of Straits Settlements Foreign Trade 1870-1915.* Singapore: National Museum.

:ams, E, Lea (1969). *The Future of the Overseas Chinese in Southeast Asia.* New York: Mcgraw-Hill Book Company.

ınathan, S (1974). *Towards a National System of Education in Singapore 1945-1973.* Singapore: Oxford University Press.

.e, HA (1966). *The Emergency in Malaya.* Penang: Sinaran Brothers Limited.

\dil, HB (1972). *Sejarah Pahang.* Kuala Lumpur: Dewan Bahasa dan Pustaka.

ırahan, GZ (1954). *The Communist Struggle in Malaya.* New York: Institute of Pacific Relations.

., AW (1974). *Nanyang Perspective: Chinese Students in Multiracial Singapore.* Hawaii: The University Press of Hawaii.

on, F (1957). *The Schools of Malaya.* Singapore: Donald Moore.

ıe, RS (1967). *Government and Politics in Malaysia.* Boston: Houghton Mifflin Company.

ıre, WK (2004). *Malaysia: A pictorial history 1400-2004.* Kuala Lumpur: Editions Didier Millet.

l History Department (1990). *Recollections: People and Places.* Singapore: Oral History Department.

vy, A (1966). *General Theory of Population.* New York: Basic Books.

:t-Ross, A (1990). *Tun Dato Sir Cheng Lock Tan.* Singapore: Alice Scott-Ross.

th, Joseph Burkholder (1976). *Portrait of a Cold Warrior.* New York: GP. Putnam's Sons.

ker, P (2001). *The No-Nonsense guide to International Migration.* UK: New Internationalist Publications.

ku Iskandar (1986). *Kamus Dewan.* Kuala Lumpur: Dewan Bahasa dan Pustaka.

aisamy, TR (1969). *150 Years of Education in Singapore.* Singapore: Teachers' Training College.

ɡonning, KG (1966). *Malaysia and Singapore.* Singapore: Donald Moore.

son, J (1958). *The Singapore Rubber Market.* Singapore: Eastern Universities Press.

, SS (1990). *Tan Cheng Lock — The Straits Legislator and Chinese Leader* Petaling Jaya: Pelanduk Publications.

of Harun (1991). *Tunku-Idealisme Dalam Kenangan.* Penang: Yayasan Bumiputra.

published Thesis

SA. Rahim, Yusoff (1960). "Malay Education in the Federation of Malaya 1945-1958", academic exercise. Singapore: University of Malaya.

ɔah KK (1956). "The Hakka Community in Singapore", academic exercise. Singapore: University of Singapore.

ɡ YH (1974). "The Politics of Chinese Education in Singapore during The Colonial Period (1911-1959)", MA. diss. Singapore: University of Singapore.

Articles

Borthwick, S (1988). Chinese Education and Identity in Singapore. In Essays in Changing Identities of the Southeast Asian Chinese since World War II, edited by Jennifer Cushman and Wang Gungwu, pp. 35–59. Hong Kong: Hong Kong University Press

James P Ongkili (1984). Darurat dan British, 1948–1960: Suatu Pernilaian. In Essays Darurat 1948–1960, edited by Khoo Kay Kim and Adnan HJ. Nawang, pp. 5–9. Ku Lumpur: Muzium Angkatan Tentera.

Justus M. Van Der Kroff (1964). Nanyang University and the Dilemmas of Overse Chinese Education. In The China Quarterly 20 (October–December), pp. 96–127.

Tregonning KG (1979). Tan Cheng Lock: A Malayan Nationalist. In Journal of Southe Asian History vol. x, pp. 25–76.

Khoo KK (1984). Gerakan Komunis di Tanah Melayu Sehingga Tertubuhnya PKM. Essays in Darurat 1948–1960, edited by Khoo Kay Kim and Adnan HJ. Nawa pp. 25–40. Kuala Lumpur: Muzium Angkatan Tentera.

Sjaastad, LA (1962). The Costs and Returns of Human Migration. In *The Journal Political Economy*, 70, pp. 80–93.

Soh, EL (1960). His Leadership of The Malayan Chinese. In Journal of Southeast Asi History vol. 1, pp. 29–55.

Tan, EJ (1977). The Singapore Rubber Market. In Singapore Rubber Centenary 187 1977, pp. 5–14. Singapore: The Rubber Centenary.

Yen, CH (1976). Chinese Revolutionary Propaganda Organizations in Singapore a Malaya, 1906–1911. In South Seas Society 29, pp. 47–67.

Index

A Retrospect on
The Dust-Laden History

THE PAST AND PRESENT OF
TEKONG ISLAND IN SINGAPORE

Chen Poh Seng's great grandfather lived in Pulau Tekong, his 50-over cousins were born and educated there. He lived in Changi Point which is 30 minutes away by ferry.

Lee Leong Sze is a Malaysian, graduated from the Department of History, National Chong Hsing University, Taiwan, and obtained a PhD in Singapore. The two researchers met in August 2005. They shared the same interest in studying the history of Pulau Tekong. During the study, they had full support and encouragement from former residents.

The book describes how Pulau Tekong developed during the early 20th century. It describes where the ethnic groups came from, how they settled down, worked and lived together, and the relationship among different ethnic groups, like the Malay and Chinese (including Hakka and Chaozhouese) over the years. Finally, the book finds out how and why the villages vanished. The final chapter outlines the outstanding citizens from Pulau Tekong and reviews how they merged with the main stream of Singapore society after leaving the offshore island.

30 YEARS
World Scientific
1981-2011

www.worldscientific.com
8234 sc

ISBN-13 978-981-4365-96-3(pbk)
ISBN-10 981-4365-96-3(pbk)

9 789814 365963